RECOVERY THROUGH DHARMA

A BUDDHIST APPROACH TO OVERCOMING ADDICTION

JIA NAVIN

Disclaimer Notice

Please note that the information contained within this document is for educational and entertainment purpose only. All effort has been executed to present accurate, up to date, reliable, complete information. No warranties of any kind are declared or implied. Readers acknowledge that the author is not rendering legal, financial, medical or professional advice. The content within this book has been derived from various sources. Please consult a licensed professional before attempting any techniques outlined in this book.

By reading this document , the reader agrees that under no circumstances is the author responsible for any losses, directly or indirectly, that are incurred due to the use of the information in this document, including, but not limited to erros, omissions, or inaccuracies

CONTENT

Introduction

As this guide will elaborate in greater detail, Recovery Dharma is not merely a program; it is a profound journey towards alleviating suffering, understanding the roots of addiction, and embracing a life infused with courage, wisdom, and compassion. Rooted in mindfulness and meditation practices, Recovery Dharma offers a unique pathway for individuals to embark upon the transformative process of recovery.

Unlike traditional recovery programs, Recovery Dharma is peer-led and peer-directed. It thrives on the collective wisdom and experiences of individuals walking the same path of recovery. Within this space, individuals have the opportunity to share, learn, and grow together, drawing strength and inspiration from one another's journeys. This guide serves as a valuable resource for those beginning their recovery journey and those seeking to sustain their progress.

It's essential to understand that Recovery Dharma isn't merely a title or a marketing gimmick; it's a lived experience. It encompasses the shared wisdom, practices, and meditations that have been cultivated through real-life struggles and triumphs. By engaging with the practices and principles outlined in these pages, individuals can tap into a wellspring of support and guidance that stems from the daily commitment of those navigating their own recovery.

Recovery from addiction is a deeply personal journey, marked by its complexities and challenges. Yet, amidst the difficulties, there is a common thread: the need for support. Recovery Dharma offers a fresh perspective and a powerful approach to addressing addiction. For those seeking an alternative to traditional recovery methods or struggling to maintain long-term sobriety, Recovery Dharma provides a beacon of hope, a sense of community, and a comprehensive framework for transforming lives and breaking free from the cycle of addiction. Through dedication, mindfulness, and the support of a community, individuals can embark on a journey towards lasting recovery and a life filled with purpose and fulfillment.

UNDERSTANDING ADDICTION

Addiction is a formidable foe, lurking in the shadows of your mind, waiting to ensnare you in its grasp. It's a relentless adversary, capable of wreaking havoc on every aspect of your life, leaving a trail of destruction in its wake.

The Nature of Addiction

At its core, addiction is a complex interplay of biological, psychological, and social factors. It's not simply a matter of weak willpower or moral failing; it's a hijacking of the brain's reward system, a rewiring of neural pathways that leads to compulsive behavior and craving. Your brain becomes wired to seek out the substance or activity that provides temporary relief or pleasure, regardless of the consequences.

Genetics also play a significant role in addiction. You may have inherited genes that predispose you to addictive tendencies, making you more vulnerable to the allure of substances or behaviors that alter your mood or perception. Environmental factors, such as exposure to trauma, stress, or peer pressure, can further fuel the flames of addiction, creating the perfect storm for its development and progression.

But addiction is not just a biological phenomenon; it's also deeply intertwined with psychological and emotional factors. It often serves as a coping mechanism, a way to numb the pain or escape from the harsh realities of life. You may turn to substances or behaviors to soothe your anxiety, ease your depression, or mask your insecurities. Over time, however, these coping mechanisms become counterproductive, exacerbating your problems rather than solving them.

Moreover, addiction thrives in isolation, feeding off the secrecy and shame that shroud its existence. You may find yourself withdrawing from loved ones, hiding your struggles, and denying the severity of your problem. This sense of isolation only deepens the grip of addiction, making it harder to break free from its clutches.

In essence, addiction is a vicious cycle, a downward spiral that traps you in a never-ending cycle of craving, consumption, and consequences. It's a relentless beast that demands constant appeasement, leaving you feeling powerless and trapped.

But here's the thing:

you are not powerless. You have the capacity to break free from the chains of addiction and reclaim your life. It won't be easy, and it won't happen overnight, but with determination, support, and the right tools, recovery is possible. You have the strength within you to overcome addiction and forge a new path forward, a path filled with hope, healing, and possibility.

Causes and Triggers

Addiction doesn't happen in a vacuum. There are underlying causes and triggers that contribute to its development and persistence. Understanding these factors is essential for unraveling the tangled web of addiction and finding your way towards recovery.

Biological Factors:

Your biology plays a significant role in shaping your susceptibility to addiction. Genetics can predispose you to addictive tendencies, influencing how your brain responds to substances or behaviors that trigger the release of dopamine, the brain's feel-good chemical. If you have a family history of addiction, you may be at a higher risk of developing addictive behaviors yourself.

Moreover, neurochemical imbalances in the brain can also contribute to addiction. Imbalances in neurotransmitters such as dopamine, serotonin, and norepinephrine can disrupt the brain's reward system, making you more vulnerable to the allure of substances or behaviors that provide temporary relief or pleasure.

Psychological Factors:

Your likelihood of developing addiction can also be affected by your psychological state. Trauma, stress, and unresolved emotional issues may lead you to seek comfort in substances or behaviors that provide temporary relief. Additionally, conditions like depression, anxiety, and other mental health disorders can heighten your susceptibility to addiction, as you might resort to substances or behaviors as a means of self-medication or managing your symptoms.

Furthermore, low self-esteem, feelings of inadequacy, and a lack of purpose or fulfillment in life can also play a role in addiction. You may use substances or behaviors to fill an emotional void or alleviate pain, only to find yourself stuck in a cycle of dependence and hopelessness.

Social and Environmental Factors:

The attitudes and behaviors towards substance use are greatly influenced by the social environment in which an individual is immersed. Peer pressure, cultural influences, and social norms all play a significant role in the formation of addictive behaviors. When individuals are surrounded by peers who partake in substance use or risky actions, they may feel compelled to conform and join in, even if it contradicts their own values.

Experiencing trauma, neglect, or abuse during childhood can elevate the likelihood of developing an addiction in the future. Adverse childhood experiences can result in enduring psychological wounds, rendering individuals more prone to adopting unhealthy coping strategies like addiction.

Triggers:

Triggers are specific cues or stimuli that elicit cravings or compulsive behaviors. They can be internal, such as stress, anxiety, or negative emotions, or external, such as being in a certain environment or socializing with certain people. Triggers can vary from person to person and can evolve over time.

Identifying your triggers is crucial for managing cravings and avoiding relapse. By recognizing the people, places, and situations that trigger your addictive behaviors, you can develop strategies for coping with them effectively. This may involve avoiding triggering situations altogether, practicing relaxation techniques to reduce stress, or seeking support from peers or professionals when cravings arise.

The Impact on Mental Health

The ravages of addiction extend far beyond the physical realm; they penetrate deep into the recesses of your mind, wreaking havoc on your mental health. Addiction can cast a shadow over every aspect of your life, leaving you feeling trapped, hopeless, and alone. Understanding the profound impact of addiction on your mental health is crucial for embarking on the journey of recovery.

Anxiety and Depression:

One of the most common effects of addiction on mental health is the onset or exacerbation of anxiety and depression. Substance abuse can disrupt the delicate balance of neurotransmitters in your brain, leading to feelings of sadness, hopelessness, and despair. Moreover, the stress and uncertainty of living with addiction can further fuel anxiety, leaving you in a perpetual state of fear and unease.

Self-Esteem and Self-Worth:

Addiction can erode your sense of self-worth and self-esteem, leaving you feeling worthless, ashamed, and undeserving of love or happiness. The cycle of addiction often involves engaging in behaviors that go against your values and beliefs, further deepening the sense of guilt and self-loathing. Over time, this negative self-talk can become ingrained, making it difficult to break free from the cycle of addiction.

Isolation and Loneliness:

Living with addiction can be an incredibly isolating experience. You may find yourself withdrawing from loved ones, avoiding social situations, and retreating into your own world of addiction. The shame and stigma surrounding addiction can make it challenging to reach out for help or connect with others who understand what you're going through. As a result, you may feel profoundly lonely, longing for connection but unable to find it amidst the chaos of addiction.

Trauma and PTSD:

For many individuals, addiction is intertwined with trauma and post-traumatic stress disorder (PTSD). Traumatic experiences from the past can serve as triggers for addictive behaviors, providing temporary relief from painful memories or emotions. However, these coping mechanisms only serve to perpetuate the cycle of addiction, making it difficult to address the underlying trauma and heal from its effects.

Cognitive Impairment:

Chronic substance abuse can impair cognitive function, affecting your ability to think clearly, make sound decisions, and solve problems effectively. You may experience memory lapses, difficulty concentrating, and impaired judgment, making it challenging to function in daily life. Moreover, the long-term effects of addiction on the brain can be irreversible, leading to lasting cognitive deficits even after achieving sobriety.

Dual Diagnosis:
Many individuals living with addiction also struggle with co-occurring mental health disorders, a phenomenon known as dual diagnosis. The presence of both addiction and mental illness can complicate treatment and recovery, as each condition may exacerbate the symptoms of the other. It's essential to address both addiction and mental health issues simultaneously to achieve lasting recovery and improve overall well-being.

In conclusion, understanding how addiction impacts your mental health is essential for taking steps towards recovery and reclaiming your peace of mind. By addressing the underlying psychological and emotional issues driving your addiction, you can break free from its grip and build a life filled with hope, purpose, and fulfillment.

THE RECOVERY DHARMA APPROACH

Imagine a path illuminated by the gentle glow of a lantern, guiding you through the darkness towards a place of serenity and healing. This is the essence of the Recovery Dharma approach—a beacon of hope amidst the shadows of addiction, offering a holistic framework for reclaiming your life and embracing a journey of transformation.

Mindfulness and Meditation

In the turbulent sea of addiction, finding a lifeline to anchor yourself can be the key to weathering the storm. Mindfulness and meditation offer just that—a sanctuary amidst the chaos, a refuge where you can find solace and strength to navigate the challenges of recovery.

What is Mindfulness?

Mindfulness is a practice of being present in the moment, fully aware of your thoughts, feelings, and sensations without judgment or attachment. It involves bringing your attention to the present moment, cultivating a sense of curiosity and openness to whatever arises.

How Does Mindfulness Help with Addiction?

Mindfulness can be a powerful tool in addiction recovery for several reasons:

1. **Increasing Awareness:**
Addiction often thrives in the shadows of unconsciousness. By practicing mindfulness, you can shine a light on your thoughts, emotions, and behaviors, becoming more aware of the patterns and triggers that fuel your addiction.

2. **Managing Cravings:**
Mindfulness teaches you to observe cravings without reacting to them. Instead of being swept away by the tide of desire, you can ride the wave of craving with curiosity and compassion, allowing it to rise and fall without succumbing to its power.

3. **Building Resilience:**
Addiction recovery is not a smooth journey; it's fraught with ups and downs, twists and turns. Mindfulness can help you cultivate resilience in the face of adversity, teaching you to stay grounded and centered amidst life's challenges.

4. **Improving Emotional Regulation:**
Addiction often coexists with emotional dysregulation, as substances or behaviors are used as a way to cope with difficult emotions. Mindfulness helps you develop healthier ways of dealing with emotions, allowing you to respond skillfully rather than react impulsively.

What is Meditation?

Meditation is a formal practice of training the mind, often involving techniques such as focused attention, breath awareness, and loving-kindness. It provides a structured framework for cultivating mindfulness and deepening your inner awareness.

How Does Meditation Help with Addiction?

Meditation can be a potent ally in addiction recovery for several reasons:

1. **Cultivating Presence:**
Meditation trains you to anchor your attention in the present moment, helping you break free from the grip of rumination and worry. By returning again and again to the breath or a focal point, you learn to cultivate a sense of presence and stillness that can counteract the restless energy of addiction.

2. **Enhancing Self-Compassion:**
Addiction often thrives on self-criticism and judgment. Meditation offers a space of unconditional acceptance and kindness towards yourself, allowing you to cultivate self-compassion and forgiveness for past mistakes.

3. **Strengthening Concentration:**
Addiction can fragment your attention, making it difficult to focus on tasks or stay present in the moment. Meditation hones your concentration skills, helping you develop the mental clarity and stability needed to resist distractions and stay committed to your recovery goals.

4. **Promoting Insight:**
Addiction is often fueled by unconscious patterns and beliefs that operate beneath the surface of awareness. Meditation offers a space for self-inquiry and reflection, allowing you to gain insight into the underlying causes of your addiction and develop a deeper understanding of yourself.

Practical Tips for Starting a Mindfulness and Meditation Practice:

- Start Small: Begin with short, manageable sessions of mindfulness and meditation, gradually increasing the duration as you build your practice.

- Find a Quiet Space: Choose a quiet, comfortable space where you won't be disturbed during your practice.

- Set a Regular Schedule: Establish a regular practice schedule and commit to sticking to it, even on days when you don't feel like it.

- Experiment with Different Techniques: Explore different mindfulness and meditation techniques to find what works best for you. Whether it's breath awareness, body scan, or loving-kindness meditation, there's no one-size-fits-all approach to mindfulness.

- Be Gentle with Yourself: Remember that mindfulness and meditation are practices, not perfection. Approach your practice with patience, kindness, and a willingness to learn from each moment.

The Four Noble Truths

In addiction recovery, finding guidance and clarity amidst the chaos can be like discovering a hidden treasure map. The Four Noble Truths offer just that—a roadmap for understanding the nature of suffering, its causes, and the path to liberation. Rooted in Buddhist philosophy, these truths provide profound insights into the human condition and offer invaluable wisdom for those navigating the challenges of addiction recovery.

#1. The Truth of Suffering:

The first noble truth acknowledges the universal reality of suffering. In the context of addiction, suffering takes many forms—it's the relentless craving for substances or behaviors, the anguish of withdrawal symptoms, the guilt and shame of past actions, and the despair of feeling trapped in a cycle of dependency. Recognizing the truth of suffering is the first step towards liberation, as it opens the door to healing and transformation.

#2. The Truth of the Cause of Suffering:

The second noble truth identifies the root causes of suffering. In the context of addiction, the causes are manifold—biological, psychological, social, and spiritual. It's the genetic predisposition to addictive tendencies, the trauma and emotional wounds that drive self-destructive behaviors, the societal pressures and cultural norms that normalize substance use, and the existential longing for meaning and purpose that goes unfulfilled. Understanding the causes of suffering empowers you to address them at their source, rather than merely treating the symptoms.

#3. The Truth of the End of Suffering:

The third noble truth offers hope in the midst of despair. It proclaims that liberation from suffering is possible—that there is a way out of the cycle of addiction and into a life of freedom and fulfillment. In the context of addiction recovery, this truth reminds you that healing is not only attainable but inevitable with the right tools, support, and mindset. It's a beacon of hope that lights the way forward, even in the darkest of times.

#4. The Truth of the Path to the End of Suffering:

The fourth noble truth lays out the path to liberation—the Eightfold Path. This path consists of eight interconnected principles or practices that guide you towards the cessation of suffering. It includes right understanding, right intention, right speech, right action, right livelihood, right effort, right mindfulness, and right concentration. Each aspect of the path offers a specific focus for your attention and effort, guiding you towards greater wisdom, compassion, and liberation.

Practical Application of the Four Noble Truths in Addiction Recovery:

- . Acknowledge the Reality of Suffering: Start by acknowledging the reality of suffering in your life—the pain, the struggles, the challenges. Recognize that suffering is a natural part of the human experience and that you are not alone in your struggles.

- . Identify the Causes of Suffering: Take a close look at the underlying causes of your addiction—biological, psychological, social, and spiritual. Explore the genetic predispositions, the traumatic experiences, the societal pressures, and the existential longings that drive your addictive behaviors.

- . Hold onto Hope: Despite the overwhelming nature of addiction, hold onto the hope that liberation from suffering is possible. Believe in your capacity to heal and transform your life, no matter how bleak things may seem.

- . Embrace the Eightfold Path: Embrace the principles of the Eightfold Path as a guide for your recovery journey. Cultivate right understanding, right intention, right speech, right action, right livelihood, right effort, right mindfulness, and right concentration in your daily life, knowing that each step brings you closer to freedom from suffering.

The Eightfold Path

In the journey of addiction recovery, finding a roadmap to guide your steps towards liberation is like discovering a treasure map in the midst of a storm. The Eightfold Path, rooted in Buddhist philosophy, offers just that—a clear and practical guide for living a life free from the shackles of addiction. Each step of the path provides invaluable guidance and wisdom for those seeking to break free from the cycle of suffering and find lasting peace and fulfillment.

#1. Right Understanding:

The first step on the Eightfold Path is cultivating right understanding—an accurate and insightful understanding of the nature of reality, including the causes and consequences of your actions. In the context of addiction recovery, this means recognizing the true nature of addiction—the causes and conditions that give rise to it, the suffering it brings, and the possibility of liberation from its grip.

#2. Right Intention:

With right understanding as your foundation, the next step is cultivating right intention—a clear and noble intention to live a life free from addiction and aligned with your deepest values and aspirations. This involves letting go of harmful intentions such as craving, ill will, and ignorance, and cultivating positive intentions such as compassion, generosity, and wisdom.

#3. Right Speech:

The third step on the Eightfold Path is practicing right speech— speaking truthfully, kindly, and skillfully, and refraining from harmful speech that causes harm to yourself or others. In the context of addiction recovery, this means being honest with yourself and others about your struggles and seeking support and guidance from those who can help you on your journey.

#4. Right Action:

Right action involves acting ethically and skillfully, refraining from harmful behaviors and cultivating wholesome actions that promote healing and well-being. In the context of addiction recovery, this means abstaining from addictive behaviors and cultivating healthy habits and behaviors that support your recovery journey.

#5. Right Livelihood:

Right livelihood involves earning a living in a way that is ethical, sustainable, and aligned with your values. In the context of addiction recovery, this may involve finding meaningful work that supports your recovery journey and contributes positively to your well-being and the well-being of others.

#6. Right Effort:

The sixth step on the Eightfold Path is cultivating right effort—making a sincere and consistent effort to overcome unwholesome mental states and cultivate wholesome ones. In the context of addiction recovery, this means applying yourself wholeheartedly to your recovery journey, practicing mindfulness, and cultivating positive mental habits that support your well-being.

#7. Right Mindfulness:

Right mindfulness involves cultivating awareness and presence in the present moment, observing your thoughts, feelings, and sensations without judgment or attachment. In the context of addiction recovery, mindfulness can help you become more aware of the triggers, cravings, and patterns that contribute to your addictive behaviors, allowing you to respond skillfully rather than react impulsively.

#8. Right Concentration:

The final step on the Eightfold Path is cultivating right concentration—developing a focused and steady mind through meditation and mental training. In the context of addiction recovery, concentration practices can help you develop greater mental clarity, stability, and resilience, allowing you to stay focused on your recovery goals and navigate the challenges of recovery with greater ease and grace.

Practical Application of the Eightfold Path in Addiction Recovery:

- **Cultivate Understanding:** Start by cultivating a clear and accurate understanding of the nature of addiction and the causes and conditions that give rise to it. Educate yourself about addiction, seek guidance from experts and peers, and reflect deeply on your own experiences and motivations.

- **Set Intentions: Clarify** your intentions for recovery and set clear, achievable goals for yourself. Identify what matters most to you and align your intentions and actions with your deepest values and aspirations.

- **Practice Ethical Conduct:** Commit to living ethically and skillfully, refraining from harmful behaviors and cultivating wholesome actions that support your recovery journey. Treat yourself and others with kindness, compassion, and respect, and avoid actions that harm yourself or others.

- **Cultivate Effort:** Make a sincere and consistent effort to overcome unwholesome mental states and cultivate wholesome ones. Practice self-discipline, perseverance, and

18

diligence in your recovery journey, and be willing to put in the time and effort necessary to achieve lasting change.

- **Develop Mindfulness:** Cultivate mindfulness in your daily life, bringing awareness and presence to your thoughts, feelings, and sensations. Practice mindfulness meditation and other mindfulness techniques to develop greater self-awareness and insight into your addictive behaviors and patterns.

- **Strengthen Concentration:** Develop concentration through meditation and mental training, cultivating a focused and steady mind that can withstand the challenges of addiction recovery. Practice concentration techniques such as breath awareness, body scan, and loving-kindness meditation to develop greater mental clarity, stability, and resilience.

PREPARING FOR RECOVERY

Preparing for recovery is not just about getting ready to stop using substances or engaging in addictive behaviors. It's about laying the groundwork for a new way of life—a life filled with purpose, meaning, and fulfillment. It's about cultivating the inner strength and resilience needed to overcome the challenges that lie ahead and embracing the possibilities that await you on the other side of addiction.

Accepting the Need for Change

Facing the reality of addiction can feel like standing at the edge of a cliff, staring into the unknown abyss below. It's a moment of reckoning, a pivotal point where you must confront the harsh truth of your situation and acknowledge the need for change. Accepting the need for change is the first step on the path to recovery—a courageous acknowledgment that opens the door to healing and transformation.

• **Understanding Resistance:**
Resistance to change is a natural human instinct, rooted in fear and uncertainty. When faced with the prospect of change, your mind may recoil, clinging to familiar patterns and habits, even if they are harmful. This resistance can manifest in various ways— denial, rationalization, minimization, or avoidance—all of which serve to maintain the status quo and resist the discomfort of change.

- **Breaking Through Denial:**

Denial is a common defense mechanism in addiction, a way of shielding yourself from the painful reality of your situation. You may minimize the severity of your addiction, downplay its impact on your life, or rationalize your behavior as being under control. Breaking through denial requires a willingness to face the truth with honesty and courage, to acknowledge the full extent of your addiction and its consequences.

- **Confronting Fear:**

Fear is another powerful barrier to change, rooted in uncertainty and the unknown. You may fear the discomfort of withdrawal, the challenges of recovery, or the stigma and judgment of others. Confronting fear requires a willingness to step into the unknown, to embrace the uncertainty of change and trust in your ability to navigate the journey ahead.

- **Finding Motivation:**

Motivation is the fuel that propels you forward on the path to change. It's the driving force that empowers you to overcome resistance, confront fear, and take action towards a better future. Finding motivation requires tapping into your deepest desires and aspirations, recognizing the value of change, and envisioning the life you want to create for yourself.

Practical Steps for Accepting Change:

1. Reflect on the Consequences: Take a honest look at the consequences of your addiction—physical, emotional, social, and spiritual. Reflect on how your addiction has impacted your life and the lives of those around you. Acknowledge the pain and suffering it has caused, and recognize the need for change.

2. Seek Support: Reach out for support from trusted friends, family members, or professionals who can offer guidance and encouragement. Surround yourself with people who believe in your ability to change and support you on your journey towards recovery.

3. Educate Yourself: Educate yourself about addiction and recovery, learning about the nature of addiction, the process of recovery, and the resources available to support you. Knowledge is empowering, and understanding the factors contributing to your addiction can help you develop a clearer perspective on your situation.

4. Set Goals: Set realistic and achievable goals for yourself, breaking down the process of change into manageable steps. Identify specific actions you can take to move towards your goals, and commit to taking consistent action towards positive change.

5. Practice Self-Compassion: Be kind and compassionate towards yourself as you navigate the challenges of change. Recognize that change is a gradual process, and that setbacks are a natural part of the journey. Treat yourself with patience, understanding, and forgiveness, and celebrate your progress along the way.

Accepting the need for change is the first step on the path to recovery—a courageous acknowledgment that opens the door to healing and transformation. By confronting resistance, breaking through denial, confronting fear, and finding motivation, you can embrace change as an opportunity for growth and create a brighter future for yourself.

Setting Goals and Intentions

Setting clear goals and intentions provides direction, motivation, and a roadmap for your journey towards healing and transformation.

Understanding Goals vs. Intentions:
Goals and intentions are closely related but serve different purposes in the recovery process. Goals are specific, measurable objectives that you aim to achieve within a certain timeframe. They provide concrete targets for your actions and progress. Intentions, on the other hand, are broader, overarching principles or values that guide your actions and decisions. They reflect your deeper aspirations and motivations for change.

The Importance of Setting Goals:
Setting goals in addiction recovery serves several important purposes:

- **Clarity:** Clear goals provide clarity about what you want to achieve and how you plan to get there. They help you break down the process of change into manageable steps and track your progress along the way.

- **Motivation:** Goals serve as powerful motivators, giving you something to strive towards and a sense of purpose and direction in your recovery journey. They provide a source of inspiration and encouragement to keep moving forward, even when the going gets tough.

- **Accountability:** Setting goals creates a sense of accountability, both to yourself and others. By committing to specific objectives, you are more likely to follow through on your actions and hold yourself accountable for your progress.

✧ **Tips for Setting Effective Goals:**

- **Be Specific:** Clearly define your goals in terms of what you want to achieve, when you want to achieve it, and how you plan to get there. Avoid vague or ambiguous goals and instead focus on concrete, actionable objectives.

- **Make Them Measurable:** Ensure that your goals are measurable so that you can track your progress and know when you've achieved them. This might involve setting specific targets, such as reducing substance use, attending a certain number of support meetings, or practicing mindfulness for a set amount of time each day.

- **Set Realistic Expectations:** Be realistic about what you can achieve within a given timeframe, taking into account your current circumstances, resources, and limitations. Set yourself up for success by setting goals that are challenging yet attainable.

- **Break Them Down:** Break larger goals down into smaller, more manageable steps to make them less overwhelming and more achievable. This allows you to focus on making incremental progress and builds momentum towards your ultimate objectives.

- **Write Them Down:** Write your goals down and review them regularly to keep them at the forefront of your mind. Consider creating a visual representation of your goals, such as a vision board or list, to serve as a constant reminder of what you're working towards.

The Power of Intentions:

In addition to setting specific goals, it's important to cultivate intentions that align with your deeper values and aspirations. Intentions serve as guiding principles that inform your actions and decisions, providing a compass to navigate the ups and downs of the recovery journey.

✧ **Tips for Cultivating Intentions:**

1. Reflect on Your Values: Take time to reflect on your core values and what matters most to you in life. Consider what you want to stand for and the kind of person you want to be, both in your recovery journey and beyond.

2. Clarify Your Aspirations: Identify your aspirations and long-term goals, beyond just overcoming addiction. What do you hope to achieve in terms of your relationships, career, health, and personal growth? Use these aspirations to inform your intentions.

3. Set Positive Intentions: Frame your intentions in positive, empowering language, focusing on what you want to cultivate rather than what you want to avoid. For example, instead of setting an intention to "stop using drugs," you might set an intention to "cultivate health and vitality."

4. Practice Mindfulness: Cultivate mindfulness as a tool for staying connected to your intentions in the present moment. Use mindfulness practices such as meditation, breath awareness, and body scan to anchor yourself in the present and align your actions with your intentions.

5. Stay Flexible: Remain open and flexible in your intentions, recognizing that they may evolve and change over time as you grow and learn. Be willing to adapt your intentions to new circumstances and insights that arise along the way.

By setting clear, specific goals and cultivating intentions that align with your values and aspirations, you can chart a course towards a brighter future and navigate the challenges of recovery with purpose and determination.

Building a Support System

In the journey of addiction recovery, you don't have to walk alone. Building a support system is like constructing a sturdy bridge—a network of connections that can help you navigate the challenges, overcome obstacles, and stay anchored on the path to healing and transformation. Your support system is your lifeline, providing encouragement, guidance, and understanding when you need it most.

Understanding the Importance of Support:

Addiction thrives in isolation, feeding off the darkness and secrecy that shrouds your struggles. Building a support system is like shining a light into that darkness, illuminating the path to recovery and creating a safety net to catch you when you fall. Your support system is comprised of individuals who believe in you, who understand your struggles, and who are committed to supporting you on your journey towards healing.

Types of Support:

1. Professional Support: This includes therapists, counselors, and addiction specialists who can provide professional guidance, therapy, and treatment to support your recovery journey. These professionals have the training and expertise to help you address underlying issues, develop coping strategies, and navigate the complexities of addiction recovery.

2. Peer Support: Peer support groups, such as Alcoholics Anonymous (AA) or Narcotics Anonymous (NA), provide a sense of community and belonging with others who have shared experiences of addiction. These groups offer a safe space to share struggles, receive encouragement, and learn

from the experiences of others who are walking a similar path.

3. Family and Friends: Your family and friends can be a vital source of support in your recovery journey. They can offer emotional support, encouragement, and practical assistance as you navigate the challenges of recovery. However, it's important to recognize that not all family and friends may be supportive, and it's okay to seek support from other sources if needed.

4. Supportive Communities: Engaging with supportive communities, whether online or in-person, can provide a sense of belonging and connection with others who are also on a journey of recovery. These communities can offer encouragement, inspiration, and practical advice for overcoming challenges and staying committed to your recovery goals.

Building Your Support System:

- **Identify Supportive Individuals:**
Take stock of your existing relationships and identify individuals who are supportive of your recovery journey. This may include family members, friends, therapists, support group members, or mentors who understand your struggles and are committed to supporting you.

- **Communicate Your Needs:**
Be open and honest with your support network about your needs and challenges. Let them know how they can best support you, whether it's through offering encouragement, providing practical assistance, or simply being a listening ear when you need to talk.

- **Set Boundaries:**
Establish healthy boundaries with your support network to protect your recovery and well-being. This may involve setting limits on the time and energy you invest in certain relationships, avoiding toxic or triggering environments, and prioritizing self-care.

- **Diversify Your Support:**
Don't rely on just one source of support—build a diverse support system that includes a mix of professional, peer, and personal support. This ensures that you have multiple avenues for support and encouragement, and reduces the risk of relying too heavily on any one individual or group.

- **Stay Connected:**
Make an effort to stay connected with your support network on a regular basis, even when you're feeling strong and stable in your recovery. Check in with your support system, attend support group meetings, and reach out for help when you need it. Building and maintaining strong connections with others is essential for long-term recovery.

Practical Tips for Building Your Support System:

- Join a Support Group: Consider joining a support group such as AA, NA, or SMART Recovery to connect with others who understand your struggles and can offer support and encouragement.

- Seek Professional Help: Reach out to a therapist or counselor who specializes in addiction treatment to receive professional guidance and support tailored to your individual needs.

- Connect with Family and Friends: Lean on supportive family members and friends who can offer emotional support, encouragement, and practical assistance in your recovery journey.

- Engage with Supportive Communities: Seek out supportive communities online or in-person, such as recovery forums, social media groups, or local community organizations, where you can connect with others who are also on a journey of recovery.

- Attend Supportive Events: Participate in recovery-oriented events, workshops, or retreats where you can connect with like-minded individuals and gain inspiration and support for your recovery journey.

Building a support system is a crucial aspect of addiction recovery, providing encouragement, guidance, and understanding as you navigate the challenges of healing and transformation. By identifying supportive individuals, communicating your needs, setting boundaries, diversifying your support, and staying connected, you can build a strong and resilient support system that empowers you to achieve lasting recovery.

DETOXIFICATION AND WITHDRAWAL

"Detoxification is the first step towards recovery—a necessary process of shedding the physical and emotional burdens of addiction in order to pave the way for healing and transformation."

Understanding the Detox Process

Detox, short for detoxification, is the process by which your body eliminates the toxic substances accumulated from substance abuse. It's a challenging but necessary phase that marks the beginning of your path towards healing and liberation from addiction.

Understanding the Purpose of Detox:

The primary goal of detox is to rid your body of the harmful substances that have accumulated as a result of substance abuse. These substances, whether drugs or alcohol, wreak havoc on your physical and mental health, impairing your cognitive function, damaging vital organs, and disrupting your body's natural balance. Detox allows your body to flush out these toxins and begin the healing process.

Types of Detox:

1. Medical Detox: Medical detox is conducted under the supervision of healthcare professionals, typically in a specialized facility or hospital setting. This type of detox may involve the use of medications to manage withdrawal symptoms and ensure your safety and comfort during the process.

2. Natural Detox: Natural detox involves abstaining from drugs or alcohol without the use of medications or medical intervention. While this approach may be suitable for some individuals with mild withdrawal symptoms, it may not be sufficient for those with more severe or complicated cases of addiction.

Understanding Withdrawal Symptoms:

Withdrawal symptoms are the body's natural response to the sudden cessation or reduction of substance use. These symptoms can vary widely depending on the type of substance abused, the duration and severity of addiction, and individual factors such as genetics and overall health. Common withdrawal symptoms may include:

- **Physical Symptoms:** These may include nausea, vomiting, diarrhea, sweating, tremors, muscle aches, headaches, and changes in appetite or sleep patterns.

- **Psychological Symptoms:** These may include anxiety, depression, irritability, mood swings, agitation, confusion, and difficulty concentrating.

- **Severe Symptoms:** In some cases, withdrawal symptoms can be severe or even life-threatening, especially for substances such as alcohol, benzodiazepines, or opioids. These may include seizures, hallucinations, delirium tremens (DTs), and respiratory depression.

Managing Withdrawal Symptoms:

The management of withdrawal symptoms during detox is a critical aspect of the process, as it can significantly impact your comfort, safety, and likelihood of successfully completing detoxification. Depending on the severity of your withdrawal symptoms and your overall health status, various approaches may be used to manage symptoms, including:

- **Medications:**
 In cases of severe withdrawal symptoms, medications may be prescribed to alleviate discomfort and reduce the risk of complications. These medications may include benzodiazepines, anticonvulsants, opioid agonists, or other supportive medications to address specific symptoms.

- **Symptom Management Strategies:**
 Non-pharmacological approaches, such as relaxation techniques, deep breathing exercises, distraction techniques, and mindfulness practices, can help you cope with withdrawal symptoms and reduce distress.

- **Hydration and Nutrition:**
Maintaining adequate hydration and nutrition is essential during detox to support your body's natural detoxification processes and promote overall health and well-being. Drinking plenty of water and consuming nutrient-rich foods can help replenish essential nutrients and electrolytes lost during substance abuse.

- **Rest and Self-Care:**
Getting plenty of rest and practicing self-care activities, such as taking warm baths, engaging in gentle exercise, and spending time in nature, can help alleviate physical discomfort and promote relaxation and healing during detox.

The Duration of Detox:

The duration of detox can vary depending on several factors, including the type and severity of substance abuse, individual health status, and the presence of co-occurring medical or mental health conditions. In general, detox typically lasts for a few days to a week, although some individuals may require longer periods of detoxification, especially if they have a history of chronic or heavy substance abuse.

Seeking Medical Assistance:

It's essential to seek medical assistance if you're considering detox, especially if you have a history of severe addiction, co-occurring medical or mental health conditions, or are at risk of experiencing severe withdrawal symptoms. A healthcare professional can assess your individual needs, provide appropriate medical care and support, and ensure your safety and well-being throughout the detox process.

By understanding the purpose of detox, recognizing common withdrawal symptoms, and seeking appropriate medical assistance, you can navigate the detox process safely and effectively, paving the way for a brighter future free from the grips of addiction.

Managing Withdrawal Symptoms

Facing withdrawal symptoms during the detox process can feel like navigating a stormy sea. But just as a skilled sailor knows how to weather the storm, you too can learn techniques to manage these symptoms and emerge stronger on the other side. Managing withdrawal symptoms requires patience, resilience, and a willingness to seek support when needed. Here's how you can navigate this challenging phase of your recovery journey:

Understanding Withdrawal Symptoms:

Withdrawal symptoms are your body's way of readjusting to life without the substances it has become dependent on. These symptoms can vary depending on the type of substance abused, the duration and intensity of use, and individual factors such as genetics and overall health. Common withdrawal symptoms may include:

- **Physical Symptoms:** Nausea, vomiting, diarrhea, sweating, tremors, muscle aches, headaches, and changes in appetite or sleep patterns.

- **Psychological Symptoms:** Anxiety, depression, irritability, mood swings, agitation, confusion, and difficulty concentrating.

- **Severe Symptoms:** In some cases, withdrawal symptoms can be severe or even life-threatening, especially for substances such as alcohol, benzodiazepines, or opioids. These may include seizures, hallucinations, delirium tremens (DTs), and respiratory depression.

✧ Tips for Managing Withdrawal Symptoms:

Stay Hydrated: Drinking plenty of water is essential during detox to flush toxins from your system and prevent dehydration, which can worsen symptoms like headaches and fatigue. Aim to drink at least eight glasses of water a day, and consider adding electrolyte-rich drinks or herbal teas to replenish lost nutrients.

1. Eat Nutrient-Rich Foods: Eating a balanced diet can help support your body's natural detoxification processes and provide essential nutrients needed for healing. Focus on whole foods such as fruits, vegetables, lean proteins, and whole grains, and limit processed foods and sugary snacks that can exacerbate mood swings and energy crashes.

2. Get Plenty of Rest: Rest is crucial during detox, as your body needs time to repair and regenerate tissues damaged by substance abuse. Aim for seven to nine hours of quality sleep each night, and consider incorporating relaxation techniques such as deep breathing exercises, meditation, or gentle yoga to promote relaxation and restful sleep.

3. Practice Self-Care: Taking care of yourself during detox is essential for managing withdrawal symptoms and promoting overall well-being. Engage in activities that bring you joy and relaxation, such as taking walks in nature, listening to music, journaling, or spending time with loved ones. Remember to be gentle with yourself and prioritize self-compassion as you navigate this challenging phase of your recovery journey.

4. Seek Support: Don't hesitate to reach out for support from friends, family members, support groups, or healthcare professionals if you're struggling with withdrawal symptoms. Talking to someone who understands what you're going through can provide validation, encouragement, and practical advice for coping with symptoms and staying on track with your recovery goals.

5. Consider Medication: In some cases, medication may be prescribed to help manage severe withdrawal symptoms or cravings during detox. These medications can help alleviate discomfort and reduce the risk of complications, allowing you to focus on your recovery journey. However, it's essential to work closely with a healthcare professional to determine the most appropriate treatment approach for your individual needs.

6. Stay Active: Engaging in regular physical activity can help distract from withdrawal symptoms, boost mood, and promote overall well-being during detox. Consider incorporating activities such as walking, jogging, swimming,

or yoga into your daily routine to release endorphins and improve your mental and physical health.

7. Practice Mindfulness: Mindfulness techniques such as meditation, deep breathing exercises, and body scans can help you stay grounded and present during the ups and downs of detox. These practices can help reduce stress, anxiety, and cravings, allowing you to navigate withdrawal symptoms with greater ease and resilience.

By staying hydrated, eating nutrient-rich foods, getting plenty of rest, practicing self-care, seeking support, considering medication when needed, staying active, and practicing mindfulness, you can effectively navigate withdrawal symptoms and emerge stronger on the other side. Remember, you are not alone in this journey, and there is hope and support available to help you overcome the challenges of detox and reclaim your life from addiction.

Seeking Medical Assistance

Facing addiction and the challenges of detox can feel overwhelming, but seeking medical assistance can be a crucial lifeline on your journey to recovery. Medical professionals are trained to provide the support, guidance, and care you need to navigate detox safely and effectively. Here's what you need to know about seeking medical assistance during the detox process:

Recognizing When to Seek Medical Assistance:

Knowing when to seek medical assistance during detox is essential for your safety and well-being. While some individuals may be able to detox safely at home with minimal medical intervention, others may require medical supervision and support to manage severe withdrawal symptoms or complications. It's essential to be aware of the signs that indicate the need for medical assistance, including:

- **Severe Withdrawal Symptoms:** If you experience severe withdrawal symptoms such as seizures, hallucinations, delirium tremens (DTs), or respiratory distress, it's crucial to seek immediate medical attention. These symptoms can be life-threatening and require prompt medical intervention to ensure your safety.

- **Co-Occurring Medical Conditions:** If you have co-occurring medical conditions such as heart disease, liver disease, diabetes, or mental health disorders, it's essential to consult with a healthcare professional before detoxing. These conditions can complicate the detox process and may require specialized medical care and monitoring.

- **History of Severe Addiction:** If you have a history of severe addiction or have previously experienced complications during detox, it's advisable to seek medical assistance to ensure a safe and comfortable detox experience. Medical professionals can assess your individual risk factors and provide appropriate care and support to mitigate potential risks.

- **Polydrug Use:** If you have been using multiple substances or have a history of polydrug use, detoxing without medical supervision can be especially dangerous. Mixing different substances can increase the risk of unpredictable withdrawal symptoms and complications, making medical assistance essential for your safety.

Benefits of Medical Assistance During Detox:

Seeking medical assistance during detox offers several benefits that can enhance your safety, comfort, and likelihood of successfully completing detoxification. These benefits include:

- Medical Monitoring: Medical professionals can monitor your vital signs, assess your withdrawal symptoms, and intervene promptly if complications arise, ensuring your safety and well-being throughout the detox process.
- Medication Management: In cases of severe withdrawal symptoms or cravings, medical professionals can prescribe medications to alleviate discomfort and reduce the risk of complications, allowing you to focus on your recovery journey.
- Individualized Care: Medical professionals can assess your individual needs and develop a personalized detox plan tailored to your specific circumstances, including any co-occurring medical or mental health conditions, substance use history, and risk factors.
- Emotional Support: Medical professionals can provide emotional support, encouragement, and guidance as you navigate the challenges of detox, helping you feel supported and empowered in your recovery journey.
- Safety Net: Having medical assistance readily available provides a safety net in case of emergencies or unexpected complications, giving you peace of mind and confidence as you embark on the journey of detox and recovery.

How to Seek Medical Assistance:

If you believe you may require medical assistance during detox, there are several steps you can take to access the care and support you need:

- **Consult with a Healthcare Professional:** Schedule an appointment with your primary care physician or a healthcare professional specializing in addiction medicine to discuss your detox needs. They can assess your individual risk factors, provide guidance on the most appropriate detox approach for your situation, and refer you to specialized treatment programs or facilities if needed.

- **Seek Outpatient or Inpatient Treatment:** Depending on your detox needs and individual circumstances, you may choose to detox in an outpatient or inpatient setting. Outpatient detox programs allow you to detox at home while receiving regular medical check-ins and support from healthcare professionals. Inpatient detox programs provide 24/7 medical supervision and support in a controlled environment, which may be necessary for individuals with severe addiction or complex medical needs.

- **Explore Medication-Assisted Treatment (MAT):** Medication-assisted treatment (MAT) combines medications with counseling and behavioral therapies to treat substance use disorders effectively. MAT can be especially beneficial for individuals with opioid or alcohol addiction, as medications such as methadone, buprenorphine, or naltrexone can help reduce cravings and withdrawal symptoms, improving your chances of successful detox and long-term recovery.

- **Reach Out to Supportive Resources:** If you're unsure where to start or need assistance navigating the healthcare system, reach out to supportive resources such as addiction helplines, support groups, or community organizations specializing in addiction recovery. These resources can provide guidance, information, and support as you seek medical assistance for detox.

Seeking medical assistance during detox is a crucial step on the journey to recovery, offering safety, support, and guidance as you navigate the challenges of detoxification. By recognizing the signs that indicate the need for medical assistance, understanding the benefits of medical supervision during detox, and taking proactive steps to access the care and support you need, you can embark on the path of detox and recovery with confidence and hope for a brighter future. Remember, you are not alone in this journey, and

help is available to support you every step of the way.

DEVELOPING RESILIENCE

"Strength does not come from winning. Your struggles develop your strengths. When you go through hardships and decide not to surrender, that is strength." - Arnold Schwarzenegger

Cultivating Self-Compassion

In your journey of recovery from addiction, cultivating self-compassion is a crucial aspect of building resilience and fostering emotional well-being. Self-compassion involves treating yourself with kindness, understanding, and acceptance, especially during times of struggle or difficulty. It's about recognizing your own worthiness of love and care, regardless of past mistakes or imperfections. Here's how you can cultivate self-compassion and nurture a more compassionate relationship with yourself:

Acknowledge Your Humanity:
Understand that as a human being, you are inherently flawed and imperfect, just like everyone else. Recognize that making mistakes and experiencing setbacks are natural parts of the human experience, and they do not diminish your worth or value as a person. Embrace your humanity with compassion and acceptance, knowing that imperfection is what makes you beautifully human.

Practice Self-Love:
Treat yourself with the same kindness and compassion you would offer to a close friend or loved one. Be gentle with yourself, especially during times of struggle or difficulty. Offer words of encouragement and support to yourself, acknowledging your

efforts and progress in your journey of recovery. Remember that you deserve love, care, and forgiveness, just like anyone else.

Challenge Self-Criticism:
Notice when your inner critic starts to speak up and fill your mind with self-critical thoughts and judgments. Challenge these negative thoughts by questioning their validity and replacing them with more compassionate and supportive self-talk. Remind yourself that it's okay to make mistakes and that failure is an opportunity for growth and learning.

Practice Mindfulness:
Cultivate mindfulness by bringing your attention to the present moment with openness and curiosity. Notice your thoughts, feelings, and sensations without judgment, accepting them as they are. When you experience difficult emotions or challenges, practice self-compassion by offering yourself kindness and understanding in those moments. Mindfulness can help you develop a more compassionate and accepting relationship with yourself.

Embrace Imperfection:
Let go of the unrealistic expectations and standards you may hold for yourself. Understand that perfection is unattainable and that striving for it only leads to self-criticism and dissatisfaction. Embrace your imperfections as part of what makes you unique and human. Celebrate your strengths and accomplishments, no matter how small, and accept your flaws with kindness and understanding.

Cultivate Gratitude:
Develop a sense of gratitude for yourself and the journey you are on. Take time each day to reflect on the things you appreciate about yourself, your progress, and your resilience. Cultivating gratitude can help shift your focus from self-criticism to self-appreciation, fostering a more positive and compassionate mindset.

Seek Support:
Reach out for support from others who understand and empathize with your struggles. Surround yourself with supportive friends, family members, or peers in recovery who can offer encouragement, validation, and understanding. Sharing your experiences and challenges with others can help you feel less alone and more supported on your journey of self-compassion and healing.

By treating yourself with kindness, understanding, and acceptance, you can build resilience, foster emotional well-being, and navigate the challenges of recovery with greater ease and grace. Remember that you are worthy of love, care, and forgiveness, and that self-compassion is a powerful tool for healing and growth on your journey to a healthier, happier life.

Building Emotional Regulation Skills

In your journey of recovery from addiction, building emotional regulation skills is essential for managing difficult feelings and maintaining stability in your life. Emotional regulation involves the ability to understand, manage, and express your emotions in healthy and constructive ways. By developing these skills, you can navigate the ups and downs of recovery more effectively and avoid relapse. Here are some practical strategies for building emotional regulation skills:

- **Identify Your Emotions:**
Begin by increasing your awareness of your emotions and learning to identify them accurately. Pay attention to the physical sensations, thoughts, and behaviors associated with different emotions. Use a feelings chart or journal to track your emotions throughout the day and notice any patterns or triggers.

- **Practice Mindfulness:**
Mindfulness is a powerful tool for enhancing emotional regulation. By practicing mindfulness, you can develop greater awareness of your thoughts and feelings in the present moment without judgment. Engage in mindfulness exercises such as deep breathing, meditation, or body scans to help you stay grounded and centered, especially during times of emotional distress.

- **Develop Coping Strategies:**
Identify healthy coping strategies that help you manage difficult emotions and reduce stress. Experiment with different techniques such as deep breathing exercises, progressive muscle relaxation, or visualization techniques to find what works best for you. Engage in activities that bring you joy and relaxation, such as spending time in nature, exercising, or listening to music.

- **Challenge Negative Thoughts:**
Learn to challenge and reframe negative thoughts that contribute to emotional distress. Practice cognitive-behavioral techniques such as thought restructuring or cognitive restructuring to challenge irrational beliefs and replace them with more balanced and realistic perspectives. By changing your thoughts, you can change how you feel and behave in response to challenging situations.

- **Build Healthy Relationships:**
Developing strong and supportive relationships can provide a valuable source of emotional support and stability in your life. Surround yourself with people who understand and respect your journey of recovery, and who can offer encouragement, empathy, and guidance when needed. Cultivate healthy boundaries in your relationships and prioritize spending time with those who uplift and empower you.

- **Practice Self-Care:**
Make self-care a priority in your life by taking care of your physical, emotional, and mental well-being. Engage in activities

that nurture and replenish you, such as getting enough sleep, eating nutritious foods, exercising regularly, and practicing relaxation techniques. Set aside time for activities that bring you joy and fulfillment, and prioritize your own needs and priorities.

- **Seek Professional Help:**
If you're struggling to manage your emotions or find yourself overwhelmed by difficult feelings, don't hesitate to seek professional help. A therapist or counselor can provide you with the support, guidance, and tools you need to build emotional regulation skills and navigate the challenges of recovery more effectively. Therapy can also help you address underlying issues or traumas that may be contributing to your emotional struggles.

By increasing your awareness of your emotions, practicing mindfulness, developing coping strategies, challenging negative thoughts, building healthy relationships, practicing self-care, and seeking professional help when needed, you can strengthen your emotional resilience and thrive in recovery. Remember that building these skills takes time and practice, but with commitment and perseverance, you can learn to navigate your emotions with greater ease and live a more balanced and fulfilling life.

Strengthening Coping Mechanisms

In your journey of recovery from addiction, strengthening coping mechanisms is essential for navigating the challenges and triggers that may arise along the way. Coping mechanisms are strategies and techniques that help you cope with stress, manage difficult emotions, and resist the urge to relapse. By developing and strengthening these coping skills, you can better manage the ups and downs of recovery and maintain your sobriety. Here are some practical strategies for strengthening your coping mechanisms:

1. **Identify Triggers:** Begin by identifying the triggers or situations that may lead to cravings or urges to use substances. Triggers can vary from person to person and may include stress, negative emotions, social situations, or environmental cues. Keep a journal to track your triggers and notice any patterns or common themes. By understanding your triggers, you can better prepare yourself to cope with them effectively.

2. **Develop Healthy** Coping Strategies: Once you've identified your triggers, develop a toolbox of healthy coping strategies that you can use to manage them. Experiment with different techniques such as deep breathing exercises, mindfulness meditation, physical exercise, or creative outlets like art or music. Find what works best for you and incorporate these coping strategies into your daily routine.

3. **Practice Relaxation Techniques:** Learn and practice relaxation techniques that can help you manage stress and reduce anxiety. Techniques such as deep breathing, progressive muscle relaxation, guided imagery, or yoga can help calm your mind and body, promoting a sense of relaxation and well-being. Incorporate these techniques into your daily routine to help you stay grounded and centered, especially during times of stress or temptation.

4. **Reach Out for Support:** Don't hesitate to reach out for support from others when you're struggling. Whether it's talking to a trusted friend, family member, sponsor, or therapist, sharing your struggles and seeking support can help you feel less alone and more supported in your recovery journey. Surround yourself with people who understand and respect your journey and who can offer encouragement, guidance, and empathy when needed.

5.   **Practice Self-Care:** Make self-care a priority in your life by taking care of your physical, emotional, and mental well-being. Engage in activities that nurture and replenish you, such as getting enough sleep, eating nutritious foods, exercising regularly, and practicing relaxation techniques. Set aside time for activities that bring you joy and fulfillment, and prioritize your own needs and priorities.

6.   **Create a Relapse Prevention Plan:** Develop a relapse prevention plan that outlines specific steps you can take to prevent relapse and cope with cravings or urges to use substances. Identify your triggers, warning signs, and high-risk situations, and create a plan for how you will respond to them effectively. Include strategies for coping with cravings, reaching out for support, and engaging in healthy alternatives to substance use.

7.   **Practice Acceptance and Mindfulness:** Practice acceptance and mindfulness by bringing your attention to the present moment with openness and curiosity. Accept your thoughts, feelings, and sensations without judgment, recognizing that they are temporary and passing. Mindfulness can help you stay grounded and centered, even in the face of difficult emotions or cravings.

Strengthening coping mechanisms is crucial for maintaining sobriety and navigating the challenges of addiction recovery. By identifying triggers, developing healthy coping strategies, practicing relaxation techniques, reaching out for support, prioritizing self-care, creating a relapse prevention plan, and practicing acceptance and mindfulness, you can build resilience and thrive in your recovery journey. Remember that building coping skills takes time and practice, but with dedication and perseverance, you can develop the tools you need to live a healthier, happier life free from the grip of addiction.

MINDFULNESS PRACTICES FOR RECOVERY

"Mindfulness is the key to unlocking the present moment, where true healing and transformation can begin."

Mindfulness can be a powerful tool for cultivating awareness, managing cravings, and finding inner peace. This practices offer simple yet profound techniques to help you stay grounded, focused, and present in the moment, allowing you to navigate the challenges of recovery with clarity and resilience.

Breath Awareness Meditation

Breath awareness meditation is a fundamental mindfulness practice that can be profoundly transformative in your journey of addiction recovery. It involves focusing your attention on the natural rhythm of your breath, serving as an anchor to the present moment and a gateway to inner peace and clarity. This practice, although seemingly simple, holds immense power to cultivate self-awareness, reduce stress, and foster resilience. Here's how to engage in breath awareness meditation effectively:

- **Find a Quiet Space:**
Choose a quiet and comfortable space where you can sit or lie down without distractions. It could be a corner of your home, a peaceful spot in nature, or anywhere you feel at ease. Create an environment that supports your practice, free from interruptions or external noise.

- **Assume a Comfortable Posture:**

Take a posture that allows you to be relaxed yet alert. You can sit cross-legged on the floor, on a cushion, or in a chair with your feet flat on the ground. Keep your back straight, shoulders relaxed, and hands resting gently on your lap or thighs. Find a position that feels comfortable for you and allows you to remain still for the duration of the meditation.

- **Close Your Eyes:**

Close your eyes gently to minimize visual distractions and turn your attention inward. This helps to deepen your focus on the sensations of your breath and enhances your ability to enter a state of mindfulness.

- **Bring Attention to Your Breath:**

Begin by bringing your awareness to the sensation of your breath as it enters and leaves your body. Notice the rising and falling of your chest or abdomen with each inhale and exhale. You may focus on the movement of air through your nostrils, the expansion and contraction of your diaphragm, or any other sensation associated with breathing. There's no need to control your breath; simply observe it as it naturally occurs.

- **Stay Present:**

As you continue to breathe, thoughts, emotions, and sensations may arise in your mind. Acknowledge them without judgment and gently guide your attention back to your breath. Each time your mind wanders, gently refocus on the sensation of breathing. This practice of returning to the breath trains your mind to stay present and cultivates mindfulness in your daily life.

- **Embrace Acceptance:**

Allow yourself to fully experience each moment as it unfolds, accepting whatever thoughts or feelings arise without resistance. Embrace the present moment with openness and curiosity, recognizing that every breath is an opportunity to connect with your innermost self and cultivate inner peace.

- **Practice Regularly:**

Consistency is key to reaping the benefits of breath awareness meditation. Set aside a few minutes each day to engage in this practice, gradually increasing the duration as you become more comfortable. Whether it's five minutes or thirty, make a commitment to yourself to prioritize your well-being and invest in your inner growth.

- **Extend Mindfulness Beyond Meditation:**

As you integrate breath awareness meditation into your daily routine, strive to extend mindfulness beyond your formal practice sessions. Bring mindful awareness to everyday activities such as walking, eating, or interacting with others. By cultivating mindfulness in all aspects of your life, you can deepen your connection to the present moment and navigate the challenges of recovery with greater ease.

Breath awareness meditation is a simple yet profound practice that can serve as a cornerstone of your journey towards healing and transformation. By dedicating yourself to this practice with patience and perseverance, you can cultivate a deep sense of inner peace, resilience, and self-awareness that will support you on your path to recovery.

Body Scan Meditation

Body scan meditation is a powerful mindfulness practice that involves systematically bringing awareness to different parts of your body, cultivating deep relaxation and heightened bodily awareness. By systematically scanning through your body from head to toe, you can release tension, reduce stress, and develop a profound sense of presence and connection with your physical self. Here's how to engage in body scan meditation effectively:

- **Find a Comfortable Position:**
Begin by finding a comfortable position to practice body scan meditation. You can lie down on your back on a yoga mat or a comfortable surface, with your arms resting gently at your sides and your legs slightly apart. Alternatively, you can sit in a comfortable chair with your feet flat on the ground and your hands resting on your lap. Choose a position that allows you to relax fully and remain still for the duration of the practice.

- **Close Your Eyes:**
Close your eyes gently to minimize visual distractions and turn your attention inward. This helps to deepen your focus on the sensations within your body and enhances your ability to enter a state of mindfulness.

- **Bring Awareness to Your Breath:**
Begin by taking a few deep breaths to center yourself and anchor your awareness in the present moment. Notice the sensation of your breath as it enters and leaves your body, allowing it to flow naturally and effortlessly. Use your breath as a guide to bring your attention into your body and prepare for the body scan meditation.

- **Start at the Crown of Your Head:**
Once you feel grounded and centered, begin the body scan by directing your attention to the crown of your head. Notice any sensations, tension, or areas of tightness in this area without trying to change or fix anything. Simply observe and accept whatever you find with a sense of curiosity and openness.

- **Progress Down Your Body:**
Slowly and methodically move your awareness down your body, scanning each part from head to toe. Pay attention to the sensations in your forehead, eyes, cheeks, jaw, neck, shoulders,

arms, hands, chest, abdomen, pelvis, thighs, knees, calves, ankles, and feet. Take your time with each part, pausing to observe any sensations that arise before moving on to the next.

- **Notice Without Judgment:**
As you scan through your body, notice any areas of tension, discomfort, or relaxation that you encounter. Approach each sensation with a non-judgmental attitude, allowing yourself to experience it fully without trying to change it. Remember that the goal of body scan meditation is not to fix or eliminate discomfort but to develop a deeper awareness and acceptance of your body as it is in the present moment.

- **Cultivate Compassion:**
As you become aware of different sensations in your body, cultivate a sense of compassion and kindness towards yourself. Offer yourself words of encouragement and support, acknowledging the challenges you may be facing and honoring the resilience of your body. Treat yourself with the same kindness and understanding that you would offer to a close friend or loved one.

- **End with Gratitude:**
As you complete the body scan meditation, take a moment to express gratitude for your body and all that it does for you. Reflect on the miraculous nature of your body's ability to heal, regenerate, and support you in your journey of recovery. Take a few deep breaths to anchor yourself in this sense of gratitude before slowly opening your eyes and returning to the present moment.

Body scan meditation is a valuable tool for cultivating mindfulness, relaxation, and self-awareness in your journey of addiction recovery. By practicing this meditation regularly, you can develop a deeper connection with your body, release tension and stress, and foster a greater sense of peace and well-being in your life.

Loving-Kindness Meditation

Loving-kindness meditation, also known as metta meditation, is a practice that involves cultivating feelings of love, compassion, and goodwill towards oneself and others. This powerful meditation technique can be particularly beneficial for individuals in addiction recovery, as it helps to foster self-compassion, reduce feelings of isolation, and cultivate a sense of connection with others. Here's how to practice loving-kindness meditation effectively:

#1. Find a Comfortable Position:
Begin by finding a comfortable position to practice loving-kindness meditation. You can sit on a cushion or chair with your back straight and your hands resting gently on your lap. Alternatively, you can lie down on your back with your arms at your sides and your legs slightly apart. Choose a position that allows you to relax fully and remain still for the duration of the practice.

#2. Close Your Eyes:
Close your eyes gently to minimize external distractions and turn your attention inward. This helps to deepen your focus on the feelings of love and compassion that you will cultivate during the meditation.

#3. Set Your Intention:
Take a few moments to set your intention for the loving-kindness meditation. You may choose to dedicate the practice to yourself, to someone you care about, or to all beings everywhere. Whatever your intention, hold it in your heart with sincerity and openness.

#4. Begin with Yourself:
Start the loving-kindness meditation by directing loving-kindness towards yourself. Repeat silently or aloud the following phrases:

"May I be happy.
May I be healthy.
May I be safe.
May I be at peace."

Repeat these phrases several times, allowing yourself to truly feel the warmth and sincerity behind each word. If you find it challenging to generate feelings of love and compassion towards yourself, be patient and gentle with yourself. Remember that self-love is a practice that takes time and effort to cultivate.

#5. Extend Loving-Kindness to Others:

Once you have cultivated feelings of love and compassion towards yourself, gradually extend these feelings to others. Start with someone you care about deeply, such as a family member, friend, or mentor. Repeat the same phrases, substituting "I" with "you" and "my" with "your":

"May you be happy.
May you be healthy.
May you be safe.
May you be at peace."

Continue to extend loving-kindness to other people in your life, such as acquaintances, colleagues, and even individuals with whom you may have difficulty. As you practice, notice any resistance or barriers that arise and allow yourself to let go of judgment and open your heart to all beings.

#6. Cultivate Universal Loving-Kindness:

Finally, expand your loving-kindness to include all beings everywhere, regardless of race, religion, or background. Repeat the phrases:

"May all beings be happy.
May all beings be healthy.
May all beings be safe.
May all beings be at peace."

Visualize sending waves of love and compassion out into the world, touching the hearts of all living beings and radiating outwards in all directions. Allow yourself to become a vessel of loving-kindness, embodying the qualities of love, compassion, and goodwill in your thoughts, words, and actions.

#7. End with Gratitude:

As you complete the loving-kindness meditation, take a moment to express gratitude for the opportunity to cultivate love and compassion in your heart. Reflect on the profound impact that this practice can have on your life and the lives of others, and commit to incorporating loving-kindness into your daily routine. Take a few deep breaths to anchor yourself in this sense of gratitude before slowly opening your eyes and returning to the present moment.

Loving-kindness meditation is a powerful tool for cultivating love, compassion, and goodwill towards oneself and others. By practicing this meditation regularly, you can develop a deeper sense of connection, empathy, and kindness in your life, fostering greater resilience and well-being in your journey of addiction recovery.

WORKING WITH CRAVINGS AND URGES

Cravings and urges are common experiences for individuals in addiction recovery, often triggering intense desires to use substances or engage in addictive behaviors. Learning how to effectively manage these cravings and urges is crucial for maintaining sobriety and preventing relapse. Here's how to work with cravings and urges in a practical and effective manner:

Identifying Triggers and Patterns

Identifying triggers and patterns helps individuals understand the underlying factors that contribute to their addictive behaviors. By recognizing these triggers and patterns, you can develop strategies to avoid or cope with them more effectively, reducing the risk of relapse and supporting long-term sobriety. Here's how to identify triggers and patterns in your journey to recovery:

1.   Recognize Common Triggers:

Triggers are stimuli or cues that evoke cravings or urges to engage in addictive behaviors. They can vary from person to person but often fall into common categories such as:

- Environmental Triggers: Certain places, people, or situations associated with past substance use or addictive behaviors.
- Emotional Triggers: Negative emotions such as stress, anxiety, depression, or loneliness.

56

- Social Triggers: Peer pressure, social gatherings, or social media interactions that promote substance use or addictive behaviors.
- Physical Triggers: Sensations in the body such as pain, fatigue, or cravings themselves.
- Cognitive Triggers: Thoughts, memories, or beliefs that reinforce addictive behaviors or cravings.

By recognizing these common triggers, you can begin to identify specific situations or circumstances that may contribute to your cravings and urges.

2.   Keep a Trigger Journal:

Keeping a trigger journal can be a valuable tool for identifying patterns and understanding your triggers more deeply. Whenever you experience a craving or urge, take note of the following:

- The date and time of the craving.
- The trigger(s) that preceded the craving (e.g., location, emotion, social situation).
- The intensity and duration of the craving.
- Any thoughts or beliefs associated with the craving.
- How you responded to the craving (e.g., coping strategies used).

Reviewing your trigger journal regularly can help you identify recurring patterns and gain insight into the underlying factors driving your addictive behaviors.

3.   Pay Attention to Physical and Emotional Cues:

In addition to external triggers, it's essential to pay attention to internal cues such as physical sensations and emotions. Notice how your body and mind respond to different situations and stimuli, and how these responses may influence your cravings and urges. For example, you may notice that stress often precedes cravings for alcohol or drugs, or that feelings of boredom trigger urges to engage in compulsive behaviors.

4.   Practice Mindfulness:

Mindfulness involves paying attention to the present moment with openness, curiosity, and non-judgmental awareness. By practicing mindfulness, you can become more attuned to your thoughts, emotions, and sensations, making it easier to identify triggers as they arise. Mindfulness techniques such as deep breathing, body scanning, and meditation can help you develop greater self-awareness and resilience in the face of cravings and urges.

5.   Seek Feedback from Others:

Sometimes, others may notice triggers and patterns in your behavior that you're not aware of yourself. Don't hesitate to seek feedback from trusted friends, family members, or members of your support network. They may offer valuable insights and observations that can help you better understand your triggers and develop strategies for managing them effectively.

6.   Reflect on Past Relapses:

If you've experienced relapses in the past, take time to reflect on the circumstances leading up to them. What triggers or situations preceded the relapse? Were there any warning signs or red flags that you overlooked? By learning from past mistakes, you can identify areas for growth and develop proactive strategies to prevent future relapses.

7.   Consider Professional Assessment:

If you're struggling to identify triggers and patterns on your own, consider seeking professional assessment and support. A therapist, counselor, or addiction specialist can conduct a comprehensive assessment of your triggers and risk factors, helping you gain a deeper understanding of your addictive behaviors and develop personalized coping strategies.

8.   Be Patient and Persistent:

Identifying triggers and patterns is an ongoing process that takes time, patience, and self-reflection. Be gentle with yourself as you navigate this journey, and remember that progress is not always linear. Celebrate your successes, learn from your setbacks, and stay committed to your recovery goals, knowing that each step forward brings you closer to a life of health, happiness, and fulfillment.

By actively identifying triggers and patterns in your addictive behaviors, you can gain greater insight into the underlying factors driving your cravings and urges. Armed with this knowledge, you can develop personalized strategies to avoid or cope with triggers more effectively, supporting your journey towards long-term sobriety and well-being.

Using Mindfulness to Navigate Cravings

In your journey towards overcoming addiction, mindfulness can be a powerful tool for navigating cravings and urges. Mindfulness involves bringing your attention to the present moment with openness, curiosity, and non-judgment, allowing you to observe your thoughts, emotions, and sensations without becoming overwhelmed by them. Here's how you can use mindfulness to navigate cravings effectively:

1.   Mindful Awareness of Cravings:

The first step in using mindfulness to navigate cravings is to cultivate awareness of your cravings as they arise. Instead of reacting impulsively to your cravings, pause and take a moment to observe them mindfully. Notice the physical sensations associated with the craving, such as tension in your body or changes in your breathing. Pay attention to the thoughts and emotions that accompany the craving, without trying to suppress or avoid them.

2.   Acceptance and Non-Judgment:

Mindfulness teaches us to approach cravings with acceptance and non-judgment. Instead of labeling cravings as "good" or "bad," simply acknowledge them as passing experiences in the present moment. Recognize that cravings are a natural part of the recovery process and that it's okay to experience them without acting on them. By adopting an attitude of acceptance towards your cravings, you can reduce the internal struggle and resistance that often intensifies cravings.

3.   R.A.I.N. Technique:

The R.A.I.N. technique is a mindfulness practice that can help you navigate cravings with greater clarity and compassion:

- Recognize: Begin by recognizing that a craving is present. Notice the thoughts, emotions, and physical sensations associated with the craving.
- Accept: Accept the presence of the craving without judgment or resistance. Acknowledge that cravings are a normal part of the recovery process.
- Investigate: Explore the craving with curiosity and interest. Notice where you feel the craving in your body and observe any underlying emotions or beliefs that may be contributing to it.

- Non-Identification: Remember that you are not defined by your cravings. Recognize that cravings are temporary experiences that arise and pass like clouds in the sky.

By practicing the R.A.I.N. technique, you can develop greater self-awareness and emotional resilience in the face of cravings.

4.   Grounding Techniques:

Grounding techniques can help anchor you in the present moment and distract you from cravings. Try engaging your senses by focusing on the sights, sounds, smells, tastes, and textures around you. Take a walk in nature, listen to calming music, or savor a cup of herbal tea. By redirecting your attention to the present moment, you can reduce the intensity of cravings and regain a sense of control.

5.   Mindful Breathing:

Mindful breathing is a simple yet powerful technique for calming the mind and body during cravings. Take a few moments to focus on your breath, noticing the sensation of air flowing in and out of your nostrils or the rise and fall of your chest and abdomen. As you breathe, allow your attention to rest fully on the present moment, letting go of any thoughts or distractions. Mindful breathing can help soothe the nervous system and reduce the intensity of cravings.

6.   Urge Surfing:

Urge surfing is a mindfulness practice that involves riding the wave of a craving without acting on it. Instead of trying to suppress or eliminate the craving, imagine yourself as a surfer riding a wave. Notice the rise and fall of the craving as it peaks and subsides, allowing it to pass naturally without resisting or indulging it. By observing the ebb and flow of cravings with mindfulness, you can develop greater resilience and self-control over time.

7.   Cultivating Compassion:

Finally, remember to cultivate compassion for yourself as you navigate cravings and urges. Addiction recovery is a challenging journey, and it's normal to experience setbacks along the way. Treat yourself with kindness and understanding, recognizing that you are doing the best you can in each moment. By practicing self-compassion, you can create a supportive inner environment that encourages growth and healing.

Incorporating mindfulness into your daily life can empower you to navigate cravings and urges with greater clarity, compassion, and resilience. By cultivating present-moment awareness and accepting your experiences without judgment, you can develop healthier coping strategies and support your ongoing recovery journey.

Developing Alternative Coping Strategies

As you navigate the challenges of addiction recovery, it's essential to develop alternative coping strategies that can help you manage cravings, cope with stress, and maintain your sobriety. While cravings and urges may be inevitable, how you respond to them can make all the difference in your recovery journey. Here are some practical and effective alternative coping strategies to consider:

- **Identify Triggers:**
The first step in developing alternative coping strategies is to identify your triggers – the people, places, emotions, and situations that often lead to cravings and urges. By recognizing

your triggers, you can anticipate challenging situations and prepare yourself to respond effectively. Keep a journal to track your triggers and reflect on patterns that may emerge.

- **Develop Healthy Habits:**
Replacing unhealthy habits with healthy ones can provide a positive outlet for stress and boredom. Engage in regular exercise to release endorphins and boost your mood. Practice relaxation techniques such as deep breathing, meditation, or yoga to reduce anxiety and promote inner calm. Eat a balanced diet rich in fruits, vegetables, and whole grains to nourish your body and support overall well-being.

- **Build Supportive Relationships:**
Surround yourself with supportive individuals who understand your journey and encourage your sobriety. Attend support group meetings, such as Alcoholics Anonymous or Narcotics Anonymous, where you can connect with others who share similar experiences. Cultivate friendships with sober peers who can offer encouragement, accountability, and understanding.

- **Find Meaningful Activities:**
Engage in activities that bring you joy, fulfillment, and a sense of purpose. Pursue hobbies and interests that you're passionate about, whether it's painting, gardening, playing music, or volunteering in your community. Finding meaning outside of substance use can help fill the void left by addiction and reinforce your commitment to sobriety.

- **Practice Mindfulness:**

Mindfulness techniques, such as mindful breathing, body scan meditation, and loving-kindness meditation, can help you cultivate present-moment awareness and cope with cravings more effectively. By bringing your attention to the present moment without judgment, you can observe cravings as passing experiences and choose how to respond to them skillfully.

- **Develop Coping Skills:**
Explore alternative coping skills that can help you manage stress, regulate your emotions, and cope with challenging situations. Practice assertive communication to express your needs and boundaries effectively. Learn problem-solving techniques to address problems proactively and find constructive solutions. Develop relaxation strategies, such as progressive muscle relaxation or guided imagery, to calm your mind and body during times of stress.

- **Create a Supportive Environment:**
Create a supportive environment that reinforces your commitment to sobriety. Remove triggers and temptations from your home, workplace, and social circle. Surround yourself with positive influences and avoid individuals who enable or encourage substance use. Establish healthy boundaries and assertively communicate your needs to others.

- **Seek Professional Help:**
Don't hesitate to seek professional help if you're struggling to cope with cravings or maintain your sobriety. Consider working with a therapist or counselor who specializes in addiction treatment. Therapy can provide you with valuable insights, coping skills, and support as you navigate the challenges of recovery.

- **Practice Self-Care:**
Prioritize self-care and prioritize your physical, emotional, and mental well-being. Get plenty of restful sleep, eat nutritious meals, and engage in activities that recharge your batteries. Practice self-compassion and treat yourself with kindness and understanding, especially during difficult times.

- **Stay Committed to Your Goals:**

Finally, stay committed to your recovery goals and remind yourself of the reasons why you chose sobriety in the first place. Keep your long-term vision in mind and celebrate your progress along the way. Remember that setbacks are a normal part of the recovery process, and each day sober is a victory worth celebrating.

By implementing these alternative coping strategies into your daily life, you can strengthen your resilience, enhance your well-being, and maintain your sobriety in the face of cravings and challenges. Remember that recovery is a journey, and each step you take towards healing is a step in the right direction.

HEALING RELATIONSHIPS

Rebuilding Trust and Communication

Rebuilding trust and communication in relationships is a fundamental aspect of the recovery process for individuals struggling with addiction. Addiction often erodes trust and strains communication, leading to misunderstandings, resentment, and conflict. However, with commitment, effort, and effective strategies, it is possible to rebuild trust and improve communication in your relationships. Here's how:

- **Acknowledge Past Harm:**
To rebuild trust, it's essential to acknowledge the harm that addiction may have caused in your relationships. Take responsibility for your actions and the impact they have had on your loved ones. Express genuine remorse and empathy for the pain and suffering you may have caused, demonstrating your commitment to change and growth.

- **Be Honest and Transparent:**
Honesty and transparency are the cornerstones of rebuilding trust. Be open and truthful in your communication with your loved ones, even when it's difficult. Share your thoughts, feelings, and experiences openly, and avoid hiding or minimizing the truth. Transparency builds credibility and fosters trust in your relationships.

- **Practice Active Listening:**
Effective communication involves not only expressing yourself but also listening actively to the perspectives and

66

feelings of others. Practice active listening by giving your full attention to your loved ones when they speak, validating their emotions, and seeking to understand their point of view without judgment or interruption.

- **Communicate Boundaries Clearly:**
Establishing and respecting boundaries is crucial for healthy communication and mutual respect in relationships. Clearly communicate your boundaries to your loved ones, and be willing to listen to and honor their boundaries as well. Boundaries provide a framework for respectful interaction and help prevent misunderstandings and conflicts.

- **Address Communication Patterns:**
Identify and address any unhealthy communication patterns that may exist in your relationships. This may include passive-aggressive behavior, avoidance of difficult topics, or excessive criticism. Work together with your loved ones to improve communication skills and develop healthier ways of expressing thoughts and emotions.

- **Practice Empathy and Understanding:**
Empathy and understanding are essential for rebuilding trust and fostering connection in relationships. Put yourself in your loved ones' shoes and try to understand their perspective, feelings, and experiences. Validate their emotions with empathy and compassion, even if you may not agree with their point of view.

- **Demonstrate Consistency and Reliability:**
Consistency and reliability are key factors in rebuilding trust. Follow through on your commitments and promises, and be consistent in your words and actions. Demonstrate reliability by showing up for your loved ones consistently and being there for them in times of need.

- **Apologize and Make Amends:**

If you have harmed or hurt your loved ones in the past, offer sincere apologies and make amends for your actions. Take responsibility for your mistakes, express genuine remorse, and demonstrate your commitment to change through concrete actions. Apologizing and making amends can help repair damage to trust and pave the way for reconciliation.

- **Seek Professional Support:**

Consider seeking professional support from a therapist or counselor to address communication issues and rebuild trust in your relationships. Individual therapy, couples counseling, or family therapy can provide you with valuable insights, tools, and strategies for improving communication and fostering healing in your relationships.

- **Practice Patience and Understanding:**

Rebuilding trust and improving communication takes time and patience. Be patient with yourself and your loved ones as you navigate the challenges of recovery and healing. Understand that rebuilding trust is a gradual process that requires consistent effort and commitment from both parties involved.

Rebuilding trust and communication in relationships is essential for individuals recovering from addiction. By acknowledging past harm, practicing honesty and transparency, actively listening, setting clear boundaries, addressing communication patterns, practicing empathy and understanding, demonstrating consistency and reliability, apologizing and making amends, seeking professional support, and practicing patience and understanding, you can rebuild trust, improve communication, and strengthen your relationships in recovery. Remember that healing takes time and effort, but with dedication and perseverance, positive change is possible.

Setting Boundaries and Prioritizing Self-Care

Setting boundaries and prioritizing self-care are vital aspects of maintaining healthy relationships and supporting your own well-being during the recovery journey. Addiction often leads to blurred boundaries and neglect of self-care, which can contribute to stress, resentment, and relapse. By establishing clear boundaries and prioritizing self-care, you can safeguard your recovery and cultivate healthier, more fulfilling relationships. Here's how:

- **Recognize the Importance of Boundaries:**
Boundaries are the limits we set to protect our physical, emotional, and mental well-being. Recognize the importance of boundaries in maintaining healthy relationships and promoting self-respect. Understand that setting boundaries is not selfish but necessary for maintaining balance and integrity in your interactions with others.

- **Identify Your Needs and Limits:**
Take time to identify your own needs, values, and limits. Reflect on what is important to you and what you need to feel safe, respected, and fulfilled in your relationships. Consider your emotional, physical, and personal boundaries, and be clear about where you draw the line in various situations.

- **Communicate Boundaries Assertively:**
Communicate your boundaries assertively and respectfully to others. Use clear, direct language to express your needs and limits, and be firm in enforcing them. Avoid apologizing or justifying your boundaries, as they are valid and necessary for your well-being.

- **Set Healthy Relationship Boundaries:**
Establish healthy boundaries in your relationships to protect yourself from harm and maintain mutual respect. This may include boundaries around communication, personal space, time commitments, and emotional intimacy. Ensure that your boundaries are consistent with your values and promote healthy interaction.

- **Practice Self-Compassion:**
Be compassionate with yourself as you navigate setting and enforcing boundaries. Recognize that it's normal to feel guilty or anxious when asserting your needs, but remind yourself that self-care is essential for your recovery and overall well-being. Treat yourself with kindness and understanding as you prioritize your needs.

- **Be Consistent in Enforcing Boundaries:**
Consistency is key when it comes to enforcing boundaries. Once you've communicated your boundaries, stick to them firmly and consistently, even if it's challenging or uncomfortable. Consistent enforcement of boundaries sends a clear message that your needs are non-negotiable and worthy of respect.

- **Practice Self-Care Regularly:**
Prioritize self-care as a foundational aspect of your recovery journey. Self-care involves taking intentional steps to nurture your physical, emotional, and mental health. This may include activities such as exercise, meditation, hobbies, spending time with supportive loved ones, and engaging in therapy or counseling.

- **Establish Healthy Routines:**
Create healthy routines that support your well-being and reinforce your boundaries. Structure your days with activities that promote balance, fulfillment, and relaxation. Stick to a regular sleep schedule, eat nourishing meals, and make time for activities that bring you joy and fulfillment.

- **Learn to Say No:**
Learning to say no is essential for maintaining boundaries and preserving your energy and resources. Practice saying no to requests or obligations that conflict with your boundaries or compromise your well-being. Remember that saying no is not a rejection of others but a prioritization of your own needs.

- **Seek Support and Accountability:**
Surround yourself with supportive individuals who respect your boundaries and encourage your self-care efforts. Lean on trusted friends, family members, or support groups for guidance, encouragement, and accountability in maintaining healthy boundaries and prioritizing self-care.

- **Practice Boundary-Setting Techniques:**
Explore various techniques for setting boundaries effectively in different situations. This may include using "I" statements to assert your needs, practicing mindfulness to stay grounded in your boundaries, and role-playing boundary-setting scenarios to build confidence and assertiveness.

- **Reflect and Adjust as Needed:**
Regularly reflect on your boundary-setting efforts and their impact on your relationships and well-being. Be willing to adjust your boundaries as needed based on changing circumstances or feedback from others. Remember that boundaries are flexible and can evolve over time to better serve your needs.

Seeking Support from Loved Ones

Seeking support from loved ones is a crucial aspect of the recovery journey from addiction. Building a network of supportive relationships can provide encouragement, understanding, and accountability, which are essential for maintaining sobriety and navigating the challenges of recovery.

71

Here's how you can effectively seek support from your loved ones:

- **Identify Your Support System:**
Identify the individuals in your life who are trustworthy, understanding, and supportive of your recovery journey. This may include family members, close friends, mentors, or members of support groups. Consider the strengths and limitations of each relationship and prioritize those who demonstrate genuine care and empathy.

- **Communicate Your Needs:**
Communicate openly and honestly with your loved ones about your recovery journey and the support you need from them. Be clear about your challenges, goals, and boundaries, and express how their support can positively impact your progress. Encourage open dialogue and invite feedback from your loved ones.

- **Set Realistic Expectations:**
Set realistic expectations for the support you can expect from your loved ones. Understand that while they may want to help, they may not always know how or may have their own limitations. Avoid placing unrealistic demands on them and appreciate the support they are able to provide, however small.

- **Be Specific in Your Requests:**
When seeking support from loved ones, be specific about the type of assistance you need. Whether it's emotional support, practical help with daily tasks, or accountability in maintaining sobriety, clearly communicate your needs and how your loved ones can best support you. Specific requests are more likely to be met effectively.

- **Express Gratitude and Appreciation:**
Express gratitude and appreciation for the support you receive from your loved ones. Acknowledge their efforts, kindness, and

understanding, and let them know how much their support means to you. Gratitude strengthens your relationships and encourages continued support from your loved ones.

- **Set Boundaries When Necessary:**
Set boundaries with your loved ones to protect your well-being and maintain healthy relationships. Clearly communicate your limits and expectations, and assertively enforce them when necessary. Setting boundaries is essential for preserving your sobriety and self-respect.

- **Practice Active Listening:**
Practice active listening when seeking support from your loved ones. Give them your full attention, validate their feelings and concerns, and respond empathetically. Listening attentively fosters trust and connection in your relationships and encourages reciprocal support.

- **Share Your Progress and Challenges:**
Share your progress and challenges with your loved ones regularly. Celebrate your victories, no matter how small, and seek guidance and encouragement when facing obstacles. Being open and transparent about your journey promotes accountability and strengthens your support network.

- **Attend Support Groups Together:**
Consider attending support groups or therapy sessions together with your loved ones. Participating in these activities as a group can deepen your understanding of each other's experiences, provide mutual encouragement, and strengthen your bonds as you navigate recovery together.

- **Be Patient and Understanding:**
Be patient and understanding with your loved ones as they navigate their own feelings and reactions to your recovery journey. Recognize that they may need time to adjust to changes

in your behavior and lifestyle, and offer them grace as they learn to support you effectively.

- **Seek Professional Help When Needed:**
If you encounter challenges in seeking support from your loved ones or if your relationships become strained, consider seeking professional help from a therapist or counselor. A trained professional can provide guidance, mediation, and tools for improving communication and resolving conflicts within your relationships.

- **Foster Mutual Support:**
Encourage mutual support within your relationships by being there for your loved ones in return. Offer a listening ear, lend a helping hand, and celebrate their successes alongside yours. Cultivating a culture of support and reciprocity strengthens your bonds and fosters resilience in both parties.

Identifying your support system, communicating your needs, setting realistic expectations, being specific in your requests, expressing gratitude, setting boundaries when necessary, practicing active listening, sharing your progress and challenges, attending support groups together, being patient and understanding, seeking professional help when needed, and fostering mutual support, you can build a strong network of support that sustains your recovery journey and enhances your overall well-being. Remember that recovery is a collaborative effort, and your loved ones can be valuable allies in your path to healing and growth.

This page was intentionaly left blank

EXPLORING RELAPSE PREVENTION

Relapse is a common concern for individuals in recovery from addiction, but it doesn't have to be inevitable. By understanding the factors that contribute to relapse and implementing effective prevention strategies, you can minimize the risk and maintain your sobriety. Here's how to explore relapse prevention:

Understanding Relapse as a Process

Relapse is often viewed as a single event, but in reality, it's a complex process that unfolds over time. Understanding this process can help you recognize the warning signs and intervene before a relapse occurs. Here's a closer look at the stages of relapse:

- **Emotional Relapse:**

In the early stage of relapse, you may experience emotional turmoil and internal struggles that increase your vulnerability to returning to substance use. These emotions may include stress, anxiety, depression, anger, or resentment. You may also engage in behaviors that jeopardize your sobriety, such as isolating yourself, neglecting self-care, or bottling up your feelings. While you may not be actively thinking about using substances, your emotional state sets the stage for further progression toward relapse.

- **Mental Relapse:**

As emotional turmoil intensifies, you may find yourself caught in a tug-of-war between your desire to remain sober and your cravings or fantasies about using substances. During this stage, you may experience internal conflicts, rationalizations, or justifications for returning to substance use. You may reminisce about the perceived benefits of using substances, minimize the negative consequences, or romanticize past drug or alcohol use. Despite your efforts to resist temptation, your thoughts increasingly focus on using substances, and your resolve begins to weaken.

- **. Physical Relapse:**

In the final stage of relapse, the internal struggle culminates in a return to substance use. At this point, you may experience a sense of powerlessness or inevitability as you succumb to your cravings and impulses. You may justify your decision to use substances, convince yourself that you can control your intake, or rationalize that a single lapse won't lead to a full-blown relapse. However, once you initiate substance use, it's difficult to stop, and you may quickly spiral back into addictive patterns of behavior.

Recognizing the Warning Signs:

Understanding the stages of relapse allows you to recognize the warning signs and intervene before a full-blown relapse occurs. Pay attention to subtle changes in your thoughts, emotions, behaviors, and physical sensations that may indicate an escalating risk of relapse. These warning signs may include:

- Increased stress, anxiety, or depression
- Difficulty managing emotions or coping with life's challenges
- Withdrawal from social support or engagement in recovery activities
- Cravings, fantasies, or preoccupation with using substances

- Rationalizations, justifications, or minimization of the risks of relapse
- Changes in sleep patterns, appetite, energy levels, or physical health
- Engaging in risky behaviors or seeking out situations associated with substance use

Intervening Early:

When you notice warning signs of relapse, it's crucial to intervene early and implement strategies to protect your sobriety. Reach out to your support network for guidance, encouragement, and accountability. Practice self-care activities that promote your physical, emotional, and mental well-being. Use coping skills, relaxation techniques, and mindfulness practices to manage stress, cravings, and difficult emotions. Stay connected to your recovery community and engage in activities that reinforce your commitment to sobriety.

Learning from Relapse:

If you experience a relapse, view it as an opportunity for learning and growth rather than a sign of failure. Analyze the factors that contributed to the relapse, identify any patterns or triggers, and adjust your relapse prevention strategies accordingly. Use the experience to strengthen your resolve, deepen your self-awareness, and refine your recovery plan. Remember that relapse is a common part of the recovery process, and it doesn't diminish your worth or your potential for long-term sobriety.

Understanding relapse as a process involves recognizing the stages of emotional, mental, and physical relapse and intervening early to prevent a full-blown return to substance use. By paying attention to warning signs, implementing effective coping strategies, seeking support from your network, and learning from relapse experiences, you can navigate the challenges of recovery with resilience and determination. Remember that recovery is a journey, and every setback is an opportunity for growth and renewal.

Recognizing Warning Signs and Red Flags

In your journey toward recovery, it's essential to be vigilant and proactive in identifying warning signs and red flags that may indicate an increased risk of relapse. By recognizing these indicators early on, you can take prompt action to safeguard your sobriety and prevent setbacks. Here's a comprehensive guide to recognizing warning signs and red flags:

• <u>Changes in Mood and Emotions:</u>
Pay attention to shifts in your mood and emotional state, as they can often serve as early warning signs of relapse. If you find yourself experiencing heightened levels of stress, anxiety, depression, or irritability, it's crucial to address these emotions proactively. Unresolved emotional distress can fuel cravings and make you more susceptible to relapse. Practice self-awareness and mindfulness to monitor your emotional well-being and intervene when necessary.

• <u>Increased Cravings and Urges:</u>
One of the most significant warning signs of relapse is a resurgence of cravings and urges to use substances. If you notice yourself obsessing over thoughts of using drugs or alcohol, or if you find yourself rationalizing or justifying substance use, it's essential to take immediate action. Reach out to your support network, engage in distraction techniques, or use coping strategies to manage cravings and resist the temptation to relapse.

• <u>Changes in Behavior and Routine:</u>
Be mindful of any deviations from your usual behavior and routine, as these can indicate underlying issues that may increase your vulnerability to relapse. If you notice yourself withdrawing

79

from social activities, neglecting self-care, or engaging in risky behaviors, it's essential to explore the root causes of these changes. Addressing these issues proactively can help you regain stability and protect your sobriety.

- Relationship Strain and Conflict:

Conflict and tension in your relationships can significantly impact your emotional well-being and increase your risk of relapse. If you find yourself experiencing frequent arguments, misunderstandings, or resentment with your loved ones, it's crucial to address these issues openly and honestly. Effective communication, setting boundaries, and seeking support from your loved ones can help alleviate relationship strain and reduce the risk of relapse.

- Isolation and Withdrawal:

Isolation and withdrawal are common precursors to relapse, as they can exacerbate feelings of loneliness, depression, and hopelessness. If you find yourself withdrawing from your support network, avoiding social interactions, or spending excessive amounts of time alone, it's essential to reach out for help. Connecting with others, participating in group activities, and seeking professional support can help combat feelings of isolation and enhance your sense of connection and belonging.

- Neglecting Self-Care:

Self-care is essential for maintaining your physical, emotional, and mental well-being in recovery. If you notice yourself neglecting self-care activities such as exercise, nutrition, sleep, or hygiene, it's essential to prioritize these aspects of your life. Taking care of your body and mind can help boost your resilience, improve your mood, and reduce your vulnerability to relapse.

- Engaging in Risky Situations:

Be mindful of the environments and situations you expose yourself to, as they can influence your risk of relapse. Avoid places, people, and activities associated with substance use, as they can trigger cravings and temptations. If you find yourself in a risky situation, have an exit strategy in place and reach out to your support network for assistance.

- Dwelling on Past Mistakes:
Ruminating on past mistakes, regrets, or failures can undermine your confidence and self-esteem, making you more susceptible to relapse. Instead of dwelling on the past, focus on the present moment and the progress you've made in your recovery journey. Practice self-compassion and forgiveness, and remind yourself that setbacks are a natural part of the process.

By remaining vigilant and attuned to the warning signs and red flags of relapse, you can take proactive steps to protect your sobriety and maintain your progress in recovery. Remember that relapse is not inevitable, and with the right support and strategies in place, you can overcome challenges and continue on your path toward lasting wellness and sobriety.

Creating a Relapse Prevention Plan

Developing a relapse prevention plan is a crucial step in safeguarding your sobriety and maintaining long-term recovery. By proactively identifying triggers, developing coping strategies, and establishing a support network, you can effectively navigate the challenges of addiction and minimize the risk of relapse. Here's a comprehensive guide to creating a relapse prevention plan:

1. Identify Triggers and High-Risk Situations:

Begin by identifying the people, places, and situations that may trigger cravings or temptations to use substances. Common triggers include stress, negative emotions, social pressures, and exposure to drugs or alcohol. Reflect on your past experiences and identify patterns of behavior that have led to relapse in the past. Once you've identified your triggers, develop strategies to avoid or cope with them effectively.

2. Develop Coping Strategies:

Equip yourself with a toolbox of coping strategies to manage cravings and navigate high-risk situations. Experiment with various techniques such as deep breathing exercises, mindfulness meditation, physical activity, journaling, or engaging in hobbies and interests. Find what works best for you and incorporate these strategies into your daily routine. Additionally, consider seeking professional counseling or therapy to learn additional coping skills and receive support.

3. Establish Healthy Habits and Routines:

Maintain a balanced and structured daily routine that prioritizes self-care, healthy habits, and positive activities. Ensure you get an adequate amount of sleep, eat nutritious meals, exercise regularly, and engage in activities that bring you joy and fulfillment. Establishing healthy routines can help stabilize your mood, reduce stress, and strengthen your overall well-being, making you more resilient to relapse.

4. Build a Strong Support Network:

Surround yourself with a supportive network of friends, family members, peers, and professionals who understand your journey and can provide encouragement, guidance, and accountability. Attend support group meetings, such as Alcoholics Anonymous (AA) or Narcotics Anonymous (NA), where you can connect with others who are on a similar path to recovery. Openly communicate with your support network about your challenges, progress, and needs, and don't hesitate to reach out for help when necessary.

5. Develop Healthy Coping Skills:

Learn and practice healthy coping skills to manage stress, anxiety, and other difficult emotions without resorting to substance use. Explore relaxation techniques such as progressive muscle relaxation, guided imagery, or yoga to help calm your mind and body. Additionally, consider cognitive-behavioral techniques such as cognitive restructuring, problem-solving, and assertiveness training to change negative thought patterns and behaviors.

6. Create a Crisis Plan:

Prepare for potential relapse scenarios by creating a crisis plan that outlines steps to take in case of an emergency. Identify trusted individuals you can turn to for support, such as family members, friends, sponsors, or therapists. Include contact information for local treatment centers, hotlines, and crisis intervention services. Having a crisis plan in place can provide you with a sense of security and empower you to take swift action if needed.

7. Monitor Your Progress:

Regularly monitor your progress in recovery and assess your adherence to your relapse prevention plan. Keep track of your triggers, coping strategies, and any relapse warning signs you may experience. Reflect on your successes and challenges, and adjust your plan as needed to better meet your evolving needs and circumstances. Celebrate your achievements and milestones along the way, no matter how small they may seem.

8. Stay Committed to Recovery:

Above all, remain committed to your recovery journey and prioritize your health and well-being above all else. Stay vigilant and proactive in managing your sobriety, and don't hesitate to seek help or support when you need it. Remember that relapse is not a sign of failure but rather an opportunity to learn and grow. Stay resilient, stay focused, and believe in your ability to overcome any obstacles that come your way.

Creating a relapse prevention plan takes time, effort, and dedication, but the rewards of maintaining sobriety and reclaiming your life are immeasurable. By taking proactive steps to protect your sobriety and surrounding yourself with a strong support network, you can confidently navigate the challenges of addiction and build a brighter, healthier future for yourself.

This page was intentionaly left blank

FINDING MEANING AND PURPOSE IN RECOVERY

Embarking on the journey of recovery from addiction is a profound and transformative experience that goes beyond merely abstaining from substances. It's about rediscovering your sense of purpose, reconnecting with your values, and finding fulfillment in life. Here's a guide to help you find meaning and purpose in your recovery journey:

Rediscovering Personal Values

In your journey of recovery from addiction, rediscovering your personal values is crucial. Your values serve as the compass that guides your decisions, actions, and ultimately, your sense of fulfillment and purpose in life. Here's how you can reconnect with your personal values:

- **Reflect on Past Experiences:**

Take a moment to reflect on your past experiences and identify moments when you felt most aligned with your values. Think about times when you felt proud of yourself, fulfilled, or at peace. What were you doing? What values were you honoring in those moments? Reflecting on past experiences can provide valuable insights into your core values and priorities.

- **Identify Core Values:**

Make a list of potential core values that resonate with you. These could include honesty, integrity, compassion, resilience, authenticity, kindness, or self-care, among others. Narrow down your list to the values that truly resonate with you on a deep level. These are the values that you want to honor and prioritize in your life.

- **Prioritize Your Values:**

Once you've identified your core values, prioritize them based on their importance to you. Consider which values are non-negotiable and which ones you're willing to compromise on. Your prioritized list of values will serve as a roadmap for making decisions and navigating challenges in your recovery journey.

- **Align Your Actions with Your Values:**

Take intentional actions that align with your core values on a daily basis. Whether it's being honest with yourself and others, showing kindness and compassion to yourself and others, or prioritizing your health and well-being, strive to live in alignment with your values. This may require making difficult choices or stepping out of your comfort zone, but it's essential for living a life of integrity and authenticity.

- **Practice Self-Reflection:**

Regularly engage in self-reflection to evaluate whether your actions and decisions are in alignment with your values. Take time to assess how you're living your life and whether you're honoring your values in various areas, such as relationships, work, and self-care. Self-reflection allows you to course-correct as needed and stay true to yourself.

- **Set Goals That Reflect Your Values:**

Set meaningful goals that are aligned with your core values and aspirations. Whether it's pursuing a career that allows you to make a positive impact, nurturing meaningful relationships, or prioritizing your mental and physical health, ensure that your goals reflect what truly matters to you. Goals that are rooted in your values are more likely to be fulfilling and sustainable in the long run.

- **Seek Support and Accountability:**

Seek support from trusted friends, family members, or mentors who can help you stay accountable to your values. Share your values and goals with them, and ask for their support and encouragement as you strive to live a life that's aligned with your values. Having a support system can provide you with the motivation and guidance you need to stay true to yourself.

- **Embrace Growth and Flexibility:**

Recognize that your values may evolve over time as you grow and change. Be open to revisiting and reevaluating your values periodically to ensure that they still resonate with who you are and who you aspire to be. Embrace growth and flexibility in your values, allowing them to adapt to your evolving needs and experiences.

- **Practice Self-Compassion:**

Be gentle with yourself as you navigate the process of rediscovering your values. It's okay to make mistakes or deviate from your values at times; what's important is that you learn from these experiences and recommit to living in alignment with your values. Practice self-compassion and forgiveness, knowing that you're doing the best you can in your journey of recovery and self-discovery.

Setting Meaningful Goals

Setting meaningful goals is a crucial aspect of your journey toward recovery and a fulfilling life beyond addiction. Meaningful goals give you direction, purpose, and a sense of accomplishment as you navigate the challenges of recovery. Here's a comprehensive guide on how to set and pursue meaningful goals effectively:

1. Reflect on Your Values and Priorities:

Begin by reflecting on your values and priorities. What matters most to you? What do you want to achieve in your life? Identifying your core values and aspirations will help you set goals that align with your beliefs and desires.

2. Make Your Goals Specific and Measurable:

Ensure that your goals are clear, specific, and measurable. Vague goals like "get better" or "find happiness" are difficult to achieve because they lack clarity. Instead, break down your objectives into tangible actions and outcomes. For example, if your goal is to improve your physical health, specify how you will do it, such as exercising for 30 minutes three times a week.

3. Break Down Goals into Smaller Steps:

Breaking down larger goals into smaller, manageable steps makes them less daunting and more achievable. Identify the actions you need to take to reach each goal and create a timeline for completing them. This approach allows you to track your progress and stay motivated as you accomplish each milestone.

4. Set Realistic and Achievable Goals:

While it's essential to challenge yourself, be realistic about what you can accomplish within a given timeframe. Setting overly ambitious goals can lead to frustration and discouragement if they're not attainable. Start with smaller, attainable goals that build confidence and momentum as you progress.

5. Focus on Both Short-Term and Long-Term Goals:

Balance your goals between short-term and long-term objectives. Short-term goals provide immediate direction and gratification, while long-term goals give you a sense of purpose and vision for the future. Having a mix of both ensures that you're making progress toward your overarching aspirations while also celebrating smaller victories along the way.

6. Write Down Your Goals and Review Them Regularly:

Document your goals in writing and review them regularly to stay focused and motivated. Writing down your goals makes them more tangible and increases your commitment to achieving them. Keep your goals somewhere visible, such as a journal or a vision board, and revisit them often to track your progress and make any necessary adjustments.

7. Stay Flexible and Adapt to Challenges:

Be prepared to adapt your goals in response to unforeseen challenges or changes in circumstances. Life is unpredictable, and setbacks are inevitable, but how you respond to them is what matters most. Stay flexible and resilient, and be willing to adjust your goals as needed to stay on track with your recovery journey.

8. Celebrate Your Achievements:

Celebrate your achievements, no matter how small they may seem. Recognize and acknowledge your progress along the way, and take pride in your accomplishments. Celebrating milestones boosts your confidence and motivation, making it easier to stay committed to your goals in the long run.

9. Seek Support and Accountability:

Don't hesitate to seek support and accountability from others as you work toward your goals. Share your goals with trusted friends, family members, or a support group, and ask for their encouragement and feedback. Having a support system can provide you with the encouragement and motivation you need to stay focused on your goals.

10. Stay Committed and Persistent:

Above all, stay committed and persistent in pursuing your goals, even when faced with obstacles or setbacks. Recovery is a journey that requires dedication and perseverance, but every step you take toward your goals brings you closer to a life of fulfillment and well-being. Keep moving forward, one day at a time, and never lose sight of the positive changes you're making in your life.

EMBRACING A BALANCED LIFESTYLE

Achieving and maintaining a balanced lifestyle is essential for your overall well-being and sustained recovery from addiction. It involves cultivating healthy habits, nurturing relationships, and finding fulfillment in various aspects of your life. Here's how you can embrace a balanced lifestyle and enhance your journey toward long-term recovery:

Nurturing Physical Well-being

Taking care of your physical health is a fundamental aspect of maintaining a balanced lifestyle and supporting your recovery journey. Nurturing your physical well-being involves adopting healthy habits, prioritizing self-care, and making choices that promote vitality and resilience. Here are practical strategies to help you nurture your physical well-being:

- **Prioritize Regular Exercise:**
Engaging in regular physical activity is essential for improving your overall health and well-being. Aim for at least 30 minutes of moderate-intensity exercise most days of the week, such as brisk walking, jogging, cycling, or swimming. Exercise not only strengthens your body but also boosts your mood, reduces stress, and promotes better sleep.

- **Focus on Nutrition:**
Fueling your body with nutritious foods is crucial for supporting your physical health and recovery journey. Aim to consume a

balanced diet rich in fruits, vegetables, whole grains, lean proteins, and healthy fats. Limit your intake of processed foods, sugary snacks, and excessive caffeine or alcohol, as these can negatively impact your energy levels and overall well-being.

- **Stay Hydrated:**

Proper hydration is vital for maintaining optimal health and functioning. Drink plenty of water throughout the day to stay hydrated and support your body's essential functions. Carry a reusable water bottle with you as a reminder to drink water regularly, and aim to consume at least eight glasses of water daily.

- **Get Adequate Rest:**

Quality sleep is essential for your physical and mental health. Aim for seven to nine hours of uninterrupted sleep each night to allow your body and mind to recharge and repair. Create a relaxing bedtime routine to promote better sleep, such as avoiding screens before bedtime, creating a comfortable sleep environment, and practicing relaxation techniques like deep breathing or meditation.

- **Practice Stress Management:**

Chronic stress can take a toll on your physical health and exacerbate cravings or triggers. Incorporate stress management techniques into your daily routine to promote relaxation and resilience. This may include mindfulness meditation, deep breathing exercises, progressive muscle relaxation, or spending time in nature. Find what works best for you and prioritize stress reduction as part of your overall well-being.

- **Schedule Regular Health Check-ups:**

Regular health check-ups and screenings are essential for detecting and preventing potential health issues. Schedule routine appointments with your healthcare provider for preventive care, screenings, and vaccinations. Be proactive in addressing any health concerns or symptoms promptly to ensure early detection and appropriate treatment.

- **Limit Substance Use:**

If you are in recovery from substance use disorder, it's crucial to abstain from using drugs or alcohol to protect your physical health and well-being. Even small amounts of substances can jeopardize your recovery and lead to relapse. Seek support from your treatment team, therapist, or support group if you're struggling with cravings or urges to use substances.

- **Incorporate Relaxation Techniques:**

Incorporating relaxation techniques into your daily routine can help reduce stress, alleviate tension, and promote overall well-being. Experiment with different relaxation techniques such as yoga, tai chi, or guided imagery to find what resonates with you. These practices can help calm your mind, soothe your nervous system, and improve your overall physical health.

- **Engage in Outdoor Activities:**

Spending time outdoors and connecting with nature can have profound benefits for your physical and mental health. Take advantage of opportunities to engage in outdoor activities such as hiking, gardening, or simply going for a walk in nature. Spending time outdoors can help reduce stress, boost your mood, and improve your overall sense of well-being.

- **Listen to Your Body:**

Pay attention to your body's signals and cues, and honor your physical needs and limitations. If you're feeling fatigued, allow yourself to rest and recharge. If you're experiencing pain or discomfort, seek appropriate medical attention. Listen to your body's wisdom and prioritize self-care to support your physical well-being.

Nurturing your physical well-being is an essential component of your recovery journey. By adopting healthy habits, prioritizing self-care, and making choices that support your physical health, you can enhance your overall well-being and resilience on the path to long-term recovery.

Remember that small, consistent actions can lead to significant improvements in your physical health and quality of life.

Prioritizing Mental and Emotional Health

Your mental and emotional well-being plays a crucial role in your overall health and recovery journey. Prioritizing your mental and emotional health involves taking proactive steps to manage stress, cope with challenges, and cultivate resilience. Here are practical strategies to help you prioritize your mental and emotional health:

- **Practice Self-Compassion:**
Self-compassion involves treating yourself with kindness, understanding, and acceptance, especially during difficult times. Instead of being self-critical or judgmental, practice self-compassion by acknowledging your struggles and offering yourself support and encouragement. Treat yourself with the same kindness and compassion you would offer to a friend in need.

- **Cultivate Mindfulness:**
Mindfulness involves paying attention to the present moment with openness, curiosity, and acceptance. Incorporate mindfulness practices into your daily routine, such as mindful breathing, body scans, or mindfulness meditation. These practices can help you become more aware of your thoughts, emotions, and sensations, allowing you to respond to challenges with greater clarity and composure.

- **Build Healthy Coping Strategies:**
Developing healthy coping strategies is essential for managing stress, anxiety, and other emotional challenges. Identify healthy coping mechanisms that work for you, such as journaling, creative expression, exercise, or spending time with supportive

95

friends or family members. Experiment with different strategies and prioritize those that help you feel grounded and resilient.

- **Seek Professional Support:**
If you're struggling with your mental or emotional health, don't hesitate to seek professional support. Reach out to a therapist, counselor, or mental health professional who can provide guidance, support, and therapeutic interventions tailored to your needs. Therapy can offer a safe space to explore your thoughts and feelings, develop coping skills, and work through challenges related to your recovery journey.

- **Practice Emotional Regulation:**
Emotional regulation involves managing your emotions in healthy and adaptive ways. Learn to recognize your emotional triggers and develop strategies for regulating your emotions effectively. This may include deep breathing exercises, progressive muscle relaxation, or practicing assertive communication to express your feelings and needs in a constructive manner.

- **Build a Supportive Network:**
Surround yourself with supportive friends, family members, or peers who understand and respect your recovery journey. Cultivate meaningful connections with individuals who uplift and encourage you, and who can provide emotional support during challenging times. Participate in support groups or recovery communities where you can connect with others who share similar experiences and challenges.

- **Set Healthy Boundaries:**
Setting healthy boundaries is essential for protecting your mental and emotional well-being. Clearly communicate your needs, limits, and boundaries to others, and prioritize self-care by saying no to activities or commitments that feel overwhelming or draining. Establishing boundaries allows you to conserve your energy and

focus on activities and relationships that nourish and support your recovery journey.

- **Practice Gratitude:**
Cultivating a practice of gratitude can help shift your focus from negative thoughts and emotions to moments of appreciation and joy. Take time each day to reflect on things you're grateful for, whether it's a supportive friend, a beautiful sunset, or a small accomplishment. Practicing gratitude can help cultivate a positive mindset and enhance your overall sense of well-being.

- **Engage in Activities That Bring Joy:**
Make time for activities that bring you joy, fulfillment, and a sense of purpose. Whether it's pursuing a hobby, spending time in nature, or volunteering in your community, prioritize activities that nourish your soul and uplift your spirits. Engaging in enjoyable activities can boost your mood, reduce stress, and enhance your overall quality of life.

Prioritizing your mental and emotional health is a crucial aspect of your recovery journey. By incorporating these strategies into your daily life, you can strengthen your resilience, enhance your coping skills, and cultivate greater overall well-being as you navigate the challenges of recovery. Remember that seeking support and practicing self-compassion are essential components of prioritizing your mental and emotional health, and that it's okay to ask for help when you need it.

Engaging in Healthy Hobbies and Activities

As you continue your journey of recovery, engaging in healthy hobbies and activities can play a pivotal role in maintaining your well-being and promoting a balanced lifestyle. These activities

97

offer opportunities for enjoyment, fulfillment, and personal growth, helping you to navigate the challenges of recovery with resilience and positivity. Here are practical strategies for incorporating healthy hobbies and activities into your daily life:

- **Choose Activities That Bring Joy:**
When selecting hobbies and activities, focus on those that bring you genuine joy and satisfaction. Consider activities you enjoyed before addiction took hold or explore new interests that pique your curiosity. Whether it's painting, gardening, playing a musical instrument, or hiking in nature, prioritize activities that resonate with your interests and values.

- **Explore Physical Activities:**
Engaging in regular physical activity is not only beneficial for your physical health but also for your mental and emotional well-being. Choose physical activities that you enjoy and that align with your fitness level and preferences. This could include walking, jogging, yoga, swimming, or participating in group fitness classes. Physical activity releases endorphins, which can improve mood and reduce stress, making it an essential component of your recovery journey.

- **Cultivate Creative Outlets:**
Creative expression can be a powerful tool for self-discovery, healing, and emotional expression. Explore creative outlets such as writing, drawing, painting, photography, or crafting. These activities offer opportunities to channel your thoughts and emotions into tangible forms of expression, allowing you to process your experiences and tap into your innate creativity.

- **Volunteer in Your Community:**
Giving back to others through volunteer work can provide a sense of purpose, connection, and fulfillment. Look for volunteer opportunities in your community that align with your interests and values. Whether it's volunteering at a local shelter, participating in community clean-up efforts, or mentoring youth,

contributing your time and skills can foster a sense of belonging and make a positive impact on others' lives.

- **Practice Mindfulness-Based Activities:**
Mindfulness-based activities, such as meditation, tai chi, or qigong, can help cultivate present-moment awareness, reduce stress, and promote inner peace. Incorporate mindfulness practices into your daily routine to enhance your overall well-being and resilience. Start with short meditation sessions or gentle movement practices and gradually increase the duration as you become more comfortable with the practice.

- **Connect with Nature:**
Spending time in nature can have profound benefits for your mental and emotional health. Take regular walks in nature, go camping, or simply sit outside and soak in the beauty of the natural world. Nature has a calming and grounding effect, helping to reduce stress, improve mood, and foster a sense of connection to something greater than yourself.

- **Cultivate Social Connections:**
Building and maintaining healthy relationships is essential for your overall well-being and recovery. Seek out opportunities to connect with supportive friends, family members, or peers who understand and respect your journey. Participate in social activities, group outings, or support groups where you can interact with others who share similar interests and experiences.

- **Set Realistic Goals:**
When incorporating healthy hobbies and activities into your routine, set realistic goals and expectations for yourself. Start small and gradually increase the frequency and duration of your activities as you build confidence and momentum. Celebrate your progress and accomplishments along the way, and don't be too hard on yourself if setbacks occur.

- **Practice Self-Compassion:**

As you engage in healthy hobbies and activities, remember to practice self-compassion and kindness toward yourself. Be gentle with yourself if you encounter challenges or setbacks, and acknowledge your efforts and progress, no matter how small. Treat yourself with the same compassion and understanding that you would offer to a friend in a similar situation.

- **Find Balance:**

Finally, strive to find a balance between work, leisure, and self-care in your daily life. Avoid overcommitting yourself or engaging in activities that drain your energy or exacerbate stress. Instead, prioritize activities that nourish and rejuvenate you, allowing you to maintain a sense of balance and well-being as you continue your journey of recovery.

By incorporating these strategies into your daily life, you can cultivate a rich and fulfilling lifestyle that supports your recovery journey and promotes overall well-being. Remember that engaging in healthy hobbies and activities is not only enjoyable but also essential for maintaining your physical, mental, and emotional health as you navigate the ups and downs of recovery.

SUSTAINING LONG-TERM RECOVERY AND ACTIVITIES

Celebrating Milestones and Achievements

Celebrating milestones and achievements is an essential aspect of your journey to long-term recovery. It serves as a reminder of your progress, resilience, and determination, while also providing motivation and encouragement to continue moving forward. Here are practical ways to celebrate your milestones and achievements:

✧   **Acknowledge Your Progress:**

Take time to acknowledge and appreciate the progress you've made in your recovery journey. Reflect on how far you've come since you began your journey to sobriety, and recognize the milestones you've reached along the way. Whether it's one day, one week, one month, or one year of sobriety, each milestone is a significant accomplishment worth celebrating.

✧   **Set Milestone Goals:**

Set specific milestone goals for yourself that align with your recovery journey. These goals can be based on the length of time you've been sober, the completion of certain recovery milestones (such as attending a certain number of meetings or therapy sessions), or achieving personal milestones related to your health, relationships, or career. Setting milestone goals gives you something tangible to strive for and provides a sense of accomplishment when you reach them.

✦　Celebrate Small Victories:

Don't underestimate the importance of celebrating small victories along the way. Whether it's resisting a craving, reaching out for support when needed, or successfully navigating a challenging situation without relapsing, every small victory is a step forward in your recovery journey. Acknowledge and celebrate these victories as they happen, and use them as motivation to continue making progress.

✦　Plan Meaningful Celebrations:

When you reach a milestone or achieve a goal, plan a meaningful celebration to mark the occasion. This could be a simple gathering with friends and family, a special meal at your favorite restaurant, or a recreational activity that you enjoy. Choose activities that align with your values and interests and that reinforce the positive changes you've made in your life through recovery.

✦　Practice Gratitude:

Express gratitude for the support, encouragement, and guidance you've received from others along your journey. Take time to thank the people who have stood by you, believed in you, and supported you through the ups and downs of recovery. Write thank-you notes, make phone calls, or simply express your appreciation in person to those who have made a positive impact on your life.

✦　Document Your Achievements:

Keep a journal or record of your achievements and milestones in recovery. Write down your thoughts, feelings, and reflections on

103

reaching each milestone, and document any lessons learned or insights gained along the way. Having a record of your progress can serve as a source of inspiration and encouragement during challenging times, reminding you of how far you've come and the obstacles you've overcome.

✧ Share Your Successes:

Share your successes and achievements with others in your support network. Celebrate your milestones publicly in support groups, recovery meetings, or online forums where you can inspire and encourage others who may be on a similar journey. By sharing your successes, you not only reinforce your own commitment to recovery but also provide hope and encouragement to others who are still struggling.

✧ Reflect on Your Growth:

Take time to reflect on the personal growth and transformation you've experienced since beginning your recovery journey. Consider how your priorities, values, and perspectives have shifted over time, and recognize the positive changes you've made in your life. Reflecting on your growth can reinforce your commitment to recovery and motivate you to continue striving for self-improvement and growth in the future.

✧ Stay Humble and Grounded:

While celebrating milestones and achievements is important, it's essential to stay humble and grounded in your recovery journey. Recognize that recovery is an ongoing process that requires continued effort, commitment, and self-awareness. Avoid becoming complacent or overconfident in your abilities, and remain open to learning, growing, and adapting as you navigate the challenges of recovery.

✧ Look Ahead with Hope:

As you celebrate your milestones and achievements, look ahead with hope and optimism for the future. Set new goals, aspirations, and dreams for yourself that reflect your ongoing commitment to living a fulfilling and meaningful life in recovery. Remember that each milestone you reach is a testament to your strength, resilience, and determination, and that there are endless possibilities for growth and success on your journey ahead.

Continuing Support and Accountability

Continuing support and accountability are crucial elements of sustaining long-term recovery from addiction. They provide you with the ongoing encouragement, guidance, and structure you need to maintain sobriety and navigate the challenges that may arise along the way. Here are practical strategies for seeking and maintaining support and accountability in your recovery journey:

1. Build a Support Network:

Surround yourself with a supportive network of individuals who understand your journey and are committed to helping you succeed in recovery. This network may include family members, friends, peers in recovery, sponsors, therapists, and support group members. Having a diverse support network ensures that you have multiple sources of support to turn to during difficult times.

2. Attend Regular Support Meetings:

Attend regular support meetings, such as Alcoholics Anonymous (AA), Narcotics Anonymous (NA), or SMART Recovery meetings, to connect with others who are also on the path to recovery. These meetings provide a safe and supportive environment where you can share your experiences, receive encouragement, and learn from others who have faced similar challenges. Make attending meetings a priority in your schedule to stay connected with your support network.

3. Work with a Sponsor or Mentor:

Consider working with a sponsor or mentor who can provide you with guidance, accountability, and support as you navigate your recovery journey. A sponsor is typically someone who has more experience in recovery and can offer you insight, advice, and encouragement based on their own experiences. Choose someone you trust and respect, and maintain open communication with them as you work together towards your recovery goals.

4. Utilize Therapy and Counseling:

Seeking therapy or counseling can be an invaluable resource for addressing underlying issues, learning coping skills, and developing strategies for maintaining sobriety. A therapist or counselor can provide you with personalized support and guidance tailored to your specific needs and challenges. Whether you prefer individual therapy, group therapy, or a combination of both, prioritize your mental and emotional well-being by investing in therapy as part of your ongoing recovery plan.

5. Engage in Peer Support Groups:

Participate in peer support groups or recovery communities both online and in person to connect with others who are also committed to sobriety. These groups provide a sense of belonging, understanding, and solidarity, and can offer valuable insights, encouragement, and accountability. Joining online forums, social media groups, or local community organizations can expand your support network and provide additional resources for staying connected in recovery.

6. Establish Accountability Measures:

Create accountability measures to help you stay on track with your recovery goals. This may include setting regular check-ins with a trusted friend, family member, or sponsor, where you can discuss your progress, challenges, and any areas where you may need additional support. Accountability measures can help you stay accountable to yourself and others, providing motivation and reinforcement for maintaining sobriety.

7. Practice Open and Honest Communication:

Maintain open and honest communication with your support network, including sharing your struggles, setbacks, and successes along your recovery journey. Communicate your needs, boundaries, and concerns clearly and respectfully, and be receptive to feedback and support from others. Effective communication fosters trust, connection, and collaboration within your support network, strengthening your overall recovery efforts.

8. Stay Connected and Engaged:

Stay connected and engaged in your recovery community by participating in activities, events, and initiatives that promote sobriety and well-being. This may include volunteering, attending sober social events, participating in recreational activities, or engaging in hobbies and interests that bring you joy and fulfillment. Staying connected to positive influences and activities reinforces your commitment to sobriety and provides ongoing support and encouragement.

9. Celebrate Progress and Achievements:

Continue to celebrate your progress and achievements in recovery, both big and small. Acknowledge your efforts, resilience, and growth along the way, and take time to celebrate your successes with your support network. Celebrating milestones and achievements reinforces your commitment to sobriety and provides motivation to continue moving forward on your recovery journey.

10. Embrace Lifelong Learning and Growth:

View recovery as a lifelong journey of learning, growth, and self-discovery. Stay open to new ideas, perspectives, and strategies for maintaining sobriety, and be willing to adapt and evolve as needed. Embrace opportunities for personal and spiritual growth, and commit to continuous self-improvement as you navigate the ups and downs of life in recovery.

By actively seeking and maintaining support and accountability in your recovery journey, you can enhance your chances of long-term success and build a fulfilling life free from addiction. Remember that recovery is a journey, not a destination, and that each step you take towards sobriety is a testament to your strength, resilience, and determination.

Embracing Ongoing Growth and Learning

In your journey of recovery from addiction, embracing ongoing growth and learning is essential for building a fulfilling and sustainable life free from the grips of substance abuse. Here are practical strategies and activities to help you continue growing and learning as you navigate your recovery journey:

✧   Cultivate Self-Awareness:

Developing self-awareness is key to understanding your thoughts, feelings, and behaviors, as well as identifying triggers and patterns that may lead to relapse. Practice mindfulness techniques, such as meditation and journaling, to cultivate self-awareness and gain insight into your inner experiences. By becoming more aware of your emotions and reactions, you can better manage stress, cravings, and other challenges in recovery.

✦   Pursue Education and Skill Development:

Invest in your personal and professional growth by pursuing education and skill development opportunities that align with your interests and goals. Whether it's completing a degree or certification program, taking online courses, or attending workshops and seminars, continuing to learn and acquire new skills can enhance your self-esteem, confidence, and employability. Identify areas of interest or passion and explore opportunities for further education and skill development in those areas.

✦   Engage in Therapy and Counseling:

Continue to prioritize your mental and emotional well-being by engaging in therapy or counseling as needed throughout your recovery journey. Therapy provides a safe and supportive space to explore underlying issues, learn coping skills, and develop strategies for maintaining sobriety. Regular therapy sessions can help you address any lingering challenges or unresolved trauma, empowering you to move forward with clarity and resilience.

✦   Explore Spiritual Practices:

Explore spiritual practices and beliefs that resonate with you, whether it's through meditation, prayer, nature walks, or participation in religious or spiritual communities. Cultivating a sense of spirituality can provide comfort, guidance, and a deeper sense of purpose in recovery. Connect with others who share similar beliefs and values, and incorporate spiritual practices into your daily routine to nurture your soul and promote overall well-being.

✧   Volunteer and Give Back:

Engage in volunteer work and community service activities to give back to others and make a positive impact in your community. Volunteering can provide a sense of fulfillment, purpose, and connection with others, while also helping you develop empathy, compassion, and gratitude. Look for opportunities to support causes that are meaningful to you and align with your values, and dedicate your time and energy to making a difference in the lives of others.

✧   Foster Meaningful Relationships:

Nurture and cultivate meaningful relationships with family members, friends, and peers in recovery who support your sobriety and personal growth. Surround yourself with positive influences who uplift and encourage you to be your best self, while also being there to offer guidance and support when needed. Invest time and effort into building and maintaining healthy relationships that contribute to your overall well-being and happiness.

✧   Set Personal Growth Goals:

Set specific, achievable goals for your personal growth and development, and create a plan to work towards them systematically. Whether it's improving your physical health, learning a new skill, or deepening your relationships, setting goals gives you direction and motivation to continue growing and evolving in recovery. Break down larger goals into smaller, manageable steps, and celebrate your progress along the way.

✧   Practice Gratitude and Reflection:

Cultivate a practice of gratitude and reflection to acknowledge your progress, blessings, and lessons learned in recovery. Take time each day to reflect on what you're grateful for and express appreciation for the positive aspects of your life. Reflect on your journey of recovery, including challenges overcome and personal growth achieved, and acknowledge the strength and resilience you've demonstrated along the way.

✧   Stay Open to New Experiences:

Remain open to new experiences, opportunities, and perspectives that can enrich your life and broaden your horizons. Step outside of your comfort zone and embrace the unknown with curiosity and openness, whether it's trying new activities, exploring different cultures, or meeting new people. By staying open to new experiences, you expand your awareness, deepen your understanding of yourself and the world around you, and continue to grow and evolve as a person.

✧   Celebrate Your Journey:

Celebrate your journey of recovery and acknowledge the progress you've made along the way. Celebrate milestones, achievements, and moments of personal growth, no matter how small they may seem. Recognize the courage, determination, and resilience it takes to overcome addiction and build a fulfilling life in recovery. By celebrating your journey, you affirm your commitment to ongoing growth and learning, and you inspire others to do the same.

Incorporating these strategies and activities into your daily life can help you embrace ongoing growth and learning in your recovery journey. Remember that recovery is a lifelong process, and each day presents new opportunities for growth, discovery, and transformation. Stay committed to your journey, stay open to learning and evolving, and continue to embrace the journey of self-discovery and personal growth in recovery.

CONCLUSION

Congratulations on completing this comprehensive guide to recovery from addiction. Throughout this journey, you've explored various strategies and activities aimed at supporting your sobriety, fostering personal growth, and building a fulfilling life in recovery. As you reflect on the insights and practical tips shared in this guide, remember that recovery is a journey, not a destination. It requires ongoing commitment, effort, and self-awareness to navigate the challenges and opportunities that arise along the way.

Reflecting on Your Journey:
Take a moment to reflect on your journey of recovery and the progress you've made thus far. Celebrate your milestones, achievements, and moments of personal growth, no matter how small they may seem. Recognize the courage, determination, and resilience it takes to overcome addiction and rebuild your life.

Continuing Your Growth and Learning:
Embrace the principles of ongoing growth and learning as you continue your journey in recovery. Cultivate self-awareness, pursue education and skill development, engage in therapy and counseling, explore spiritual practices, and foster meaningful relationships. Set personal growth goals, practice gratitude and reflection, stay open to new experiences, and celebrate your journey of recovery.

Sustaining Long-Term Recovery:
Sustaining long-term recovery requires dedication, perseverance, and a commitment to prioritizing your physical, mental, and emotional well-being. Stay connected to your support network, seek help when needed, and engage in activities that promote a

balanced and healthy lifestyle. Celebrate your achievements, remain accountable to your goals, and embrace ongoing growth and learning as integral parts of your recovery journey.

Final Thoughts

Remember that recovery is a journey of self-discovery and personal transformation. It's okay to face challenges and setbacks along the way, as they provide opportunities for growth and learning. Stay resilient, stay focused on your goals, and never lose sight of the progress you've made. You are capable of creating a fulfilling and meaningful life in recovery, one step at a time.

As you continue on your journey, know that you are not alone. There is support, guidance, and encouragement available to you every step of the way. Reach out to your support network, seek professional help when needed, and never hesitate to ask for assistance. Your journey of recovery is unique to you, and your experiences and insights can inspire and empower others on their own paths to healing.

Above all, remember that you are worthy of a life filled with joy, purpose, and fulfillment. Believe in yourself, trust in your resilience, and embrace the journey of recovery with courage and determination. You have the strength within you to overcome any obstacle and create the life you desire. Keep moving forward, one day at a time, and never lose hope in the power of recovery.

With determination and perseverance, you can overcome addiction and embrace a brighter future filled with hope and possibility. Your journey of recovery is a testament to your strength, resilience, and unwavering commitment to creating a life of meaning and purpose. Keep shining your light and inspiring others along the way. Your recovery journey is a testament to your courage, strength, and resilience. Keep moving forward with hope, determination, and the knowledge that you are never alone on this journey.

Made in United States
Troutdale, OR
03/06/2025

29546532R00069